HOW TO RAISE KIDS WHO WON'T HATE YOU

HOW TO RAISE KIDS WHO WON'T HATE YOU

BRINGING UP ROCKSTARS AND OTHER FORMS OF CHILDREN

ALAN THICKE

STERLING & ROSS PUBLISHERS

NEW YORK

Published by

STERLING & ROSS PUBLISHERS

New York, NY 10001
www.sterlingandross.com

Library of Congress Cataloging-in-Publication Data

Thicke, Alan.
How to raise kids who won't hate you / by Alan Thicke.
p. cm.
ISBN 978-0-9814535-3-8 (pbk.)
1. Parenting. 2. Parent and child. 3. Parenting--Humor. 4. Child rearing--Humor. I. Title.
HQ755.8.T54 2008
649'.1--dc22
2008042622

Design: *the*BookDesigners
Book editor: Rachel Trusheim

10 9 8 7 6 5 4 3 2 1

Printed in the United States of America.

To my mother, Joan Shirley Isabel Greer Thicke.
She should have been with us longer. Everyone needs a mom.

To my dad, Dr. Brian Christopher Thicke,
the brunt of some "hated" moments early on, completely appreciated later.

CONTENTS

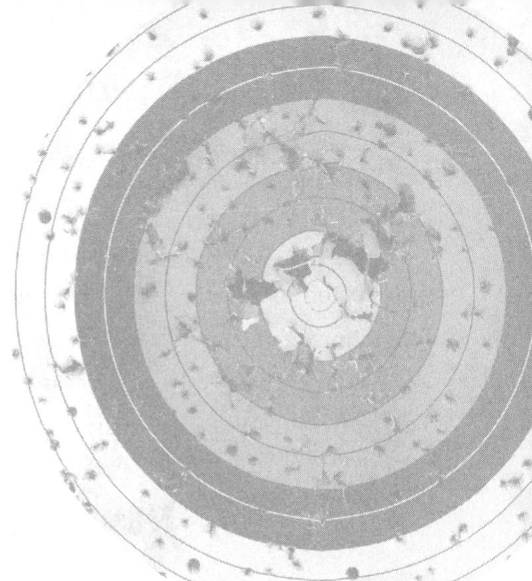

Mission Statement

"WHAT'S THIS BOOK ABOUT, ANYWAY?" YOU MAY WELL ASK, GIVEN you've possibly never read me before. By way of explanation, it may be helpful to list the other titles we considered:

- *How to Raise a Kid Like You, Only Better*
- *Scary Things They Don't Tell You About Children*

But we settled on *How to Raise Kids Who Won't Hate You* because that, after all, is what many of us live for: nurturing decent, healthy, happy children who grow up in our image (sort of), stay out of trouble (mostly), and still love us unconditionally at the end of the day because of our bond and in spite of our annoying qualities.

Thanks for buying this book, but I have to admit, the title is bogus. It's a lie. A false premise. Can't happen. Your children will hate you. Maybe not completely, and possibly not for long, but sometime, somehow, and for some reason, you will be the object of their all-consuming enmity and rage. You are the one blocking their path to the cookie jar, no matter what's in that jar. OK, maybe hate is too strong a word, but it's a word that appears in many Li'l Wayne songs, and if you don't know who Li'l is, you're probably already in trouble with your fifteen-year-old. It's important that you keep the sizzle and not fizzle with the kizzle when his schnizzle's in a pizzle. If you understand that, you'll be all right, give or take a few brain cells. (That was inspired by Snoop Dogg. I'm always happy to credit other authors.)

MOMMY DEAREST

DO YOU REMEMBER THE MOMENT YOU FIRST HATED YOUR PARENTS? That instant? That day? That year?

You hated them because they said "no" a lot—or maybe one time in particular—and you vowed that when it was your turn you'd be nicer, because the last thing you would want would be for your kids to loathe you.

We aim to change the things we think were mistakes by the previous generation. This is known as Bush's Law: George Jr. knew he should go after Saddam because his dad did not. OK, bad example.

An extreme makeover of your parents' style is rarely necessary—what's important is to keep their good traits in the gene pool while eliminating the things that bugged you. However, the love we want from our kids is so important that we as moms and dads sometimes make bad judgments to ensure we get that love.

AMA? FDA? MSNBC?

IT'S A FULL-TIME JOB KEEPING UP WITH THE EXPERTS, SINCE THEY change their minds about as often as the rest of us change our socks. In the 1890s, Dr. Luther Emmett Holt's recommendations included that children should dine at an early hour on mashed, strained, or boiled foods—nothing fresh, nothing colorful, nothing flavorful. (Evidently, he knew my mom.)

By the 1920s, John B. Watson dug deeper and advised that (1) you never let children sit on your lap and (2) when you say goodnight, kiss them once on the forehead.

Holt also recommended ignoring the advice of grandmothers, as they are notorious front-runners who invariably side with the kids. You have a better chance of getting an unbiased opinion from Fox News or an under-tipped cabbie.

In the '50s, Dr. Benjamin Spock, America's first true pop-Freudian guru, urged mothers to loosen up and to get in touch with their feelings as well as those of their children. He said that because kids don't come with an operator's manual, parents must learn to trust their instincts.

These days, we are often paralyzed by too much information and cannot consistently make confident decisions without a counselor, teacher, pediatrician, nutritionist, or Mommies Group. Thousands of advisors have been heard from since Dr. Spock and now you have me, and I'm glad to be of service. I've rounded up data on your behalf from doctors, psychologists, philosophers, and in some cases simply outspoken, opinionated loudmouths—you know who you are. Everything else will be rumor or hearsay, along with my own smart-ass remarks.

I thought of consulting several celebrities, because the American public never seems to tire of hearing what famous people have to say whether or not they have a clue about the subject. Unfortunately, as soon as we embrace a shining star, he does something stupid or illegal, and suddenly I'm stuck with a book full of parenting tips from felons. Besides, the first people I called for family-friendly advice didn't call me back, and I figured I might spend forever getting nowhere. That was Jon and Kate. You're welcome to try them yourself. On second thought, I think I got a "number no longer in service" recording.

IT'S DAD-HEAVY

MY POINT OF VIEW WILL BE DECIDEDLY MALE BECAUSE WE ARE commonly assumed to be the gender most in need of enlightenment. I'll mostly refer to your child as "he" simply because that's easier for me as the father of three boys.

I may even quote myself inadvertently—or advertently—since my own opinion is often my favorite. My previous book, an insightful effort called *How Men Have Babies: The Pregnant Father's Survival Guide*, is eminently quotable. You'll find that my level of confidence, however tenuously justified, will come in handy in your role as a parent. A sense of authority will be important when trying to convince your kids that you are right, even when you're just winging it. That will buy you time to look up the right answer.

Let me also boast that my credentials include a Doctorate of Banquetry, having matriculated in boiled chicken on the lecture circuit, where I have spoken at healthcare and parenting fundraisers and risked salmonella to do it. I'm always attentive to other speakers, so every dinner has been a seminar for me as well, and I've learned much at these events, including how to be the first to get up and go to my car.

WHAT TO DO WHEN YOUR BABY CRIES

DO YOU:

a) Cry with him, only louder?
b) Have an alcoholic beverage?
c) Ignore him until he's ten?

If you answered "yes" to any of the above, you're my kind of people, and we'll have a good time together in the silly parts. I will try not to insult your intelligence with too much common-sense claptrap. Many parenting books seem to be aimed at people apparently so dim it's a wonder they got the conception part right (i.e., Step 1: Douse yourself with cologne, Step 2: Lie down somewhere bouncy, Step 3: Find a partner before beginning Step 1, etc.).

WHO YA GONNA CALL, GHOSTBUSTERS?

THERE EXISTS A BLACK HOLE, A TROUBLING VOID, IN THE "preventive maintenance" area of parenting instruction. We have plenty of remedial and rehabilitative options, from guidance counselors to pastors, child services to the prison system, but where do we turn to for advice (reruns of *Growing Pains* aside) before serious problems arise? You can choke on a chicken bone and have a paramedic at the door in minutes or call a fireman to get a cat out of a tree, but whom do you call when your kid says "no" to everything? I would prefer that you not call me, on the assumption that everything I know came from a T-shirt or a bumper sticker and is covered in these pages. Or, you could try Jon and Kate again. But don't you wish you had an organized, systematic approach for staying ahead of the curve and avoiding trouble?

I've always believed there should be courses in high school on marital relations—what to expect and how to make it work—followed by a curriculum on how to be a family. Bravo for English lit and math, but more students will grow up to be parents than to be Stephen Kings or Stephen Hawkings, so let's spend time preparing our youth for those roles, too.

To quote myself—I just couldn't wait any longer—if this is the only book you read on child-rearing, I'm flattered and you're screwed.

Other published works will describe the incomparable joys of parenting, and I concur completely. There are thousands—no, millions—of fabulous things about raising your child that will entertain and amuse you, fill your heart, and move you to thank God for your good fortune in creating this angel.

But my mandate this time around is not to celebrate those self-evident pleasures. I'm here to talk about the dark side.

In warding off the Evil Empire of Influential Forces, I will remind you that the Temptations were more than a Motown group.

There's a problem child at every gathering, and your job is to make sure it's not yours. Remember this one? (It's from the Bible, so you'd better say "yes.")

Absalom murdered his half-brother Ammon for raping their sister Tamar, and then he slept with his father's concubine and had himself declared King of Israel while his father still reigned. Dr. Phil would have a field day with this guy.

Ultimately, Absalom got his hair caught in a tree during a battle and was killed by King David's men. Odds are this won't happen in your family, but you must know what to do in every situation. OK, I can't think of every situation and neither can you; not even the Library of Congress has enough material to anticipate the surprises you'll encounter. That's why the concept of Defensive Parenting is important. You must recognize that (1) there are outside influences on your child that you'd prefer did not exist and that (2) the best way to handle them is to be a Defensive Parent.

Psychologists tell us we are our child's primary influence until age five, at which time the peer group gains a toehold. From then on, it's a splintered universe.

Against the Evil Empire, you need to do four positives: anticipate, educate, infiltrate, and terminate.

You'll be glad you did.

P.S.

ABBY'S TOMB HAS BEEN STONED BY PASSERSBY FOR 400 YEARS, AND dads take their sons to view the stoning as a rite of passage, noting, "This is what happens when you don't listen to your father." To summarize, my objective is to share information while making you laugh along the way, aiming for something between Dr. Phil and Dave Barry. I'll occasionally drop snippets of data in short paragraphs or in point form—the short attention span approach. These random but brief digressions will be on items I find interesting. I hope you'll agree and wander with me. If you get to a chapter that seems to be all about infants and you're already past potty training, you may want to skip ahead to a section about the older kids you're wrestling with. Good luck to both of us, and let's begin.

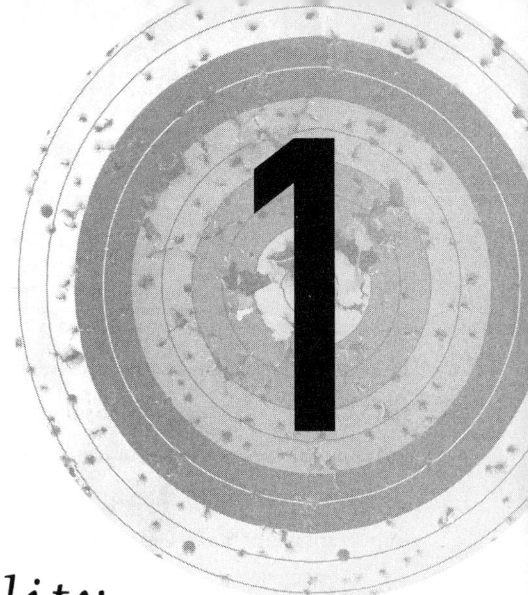

Responsibility

"Honey, I Screwed Up the Kids!"

THERE ARE WAYS, TO BE SURE, THAT YOU CAN GUARANTEE YOUR children's never-ending love.

Money—*Buy them everything they want.*
Food—*Feed them nothing but cookies.*
Education—*Tell them homework is for cowards.*
TV—*Make sure they watch a lot of cartoons.*
Sex—*Set aside a cozy place in the den for the little girl you call "Pumpkin" to get busy with the quarterback.*
Morals—*Optional.*
Manners—*See Morals.*

They won't hate you if you let them talk back as children, make their own rules as preteens, then stay out as late as they want, drink more beer than they can handle, have as much sex as they can get their hands on, sneak into clubs, drive drunk, and miss their court dates. When they drop out of school, you can buy them a car and cosign for their apartment. Then find the unemployable slug an entry-level position in your firm and let him come home to trash the house when you're out of town and move back in when your first grandchild is born out of wedlock. Your kids will indeed love you—or at least the lifestyle—until they sober up, that is, until they realize they have no ability to function in society because you have taught them only about life from A to B.

Is this starting to sound cynical? Good. Cynicism and paranoia are important elements in Defensive Parenting.

MULTIPLE DEFENSES

FOOTBALL FANS WILL RECOGNIZE THE NEED TO KEEP THE OTHER team guessing with a variety of "looks," strategies, and formations. As a parent, you must use your entire arsenal of socio-psychological tricks and tools, which must include the following:

Bribery—*Offer goods and services and other "soft money" when cash and merchandise would be too obvious.*
Chicanery—*Practice deceit to keep you on an equal footing. Spying is good.*
Skullduggery—*Chicanery for pirates.*
Tomfoolery—*Keep "lightness" in the mix.*
Sagacity—*Be smarter than they are. A long shot.*
Felicity—*I don't know what this means, although she's a darn good actress.*
Temerity—*Like felicity (but not so much with the acting).*
Punctuality—*Don't be late for this one.*
Solidarity—*Be on the same page as the other parent. This is a big one.*
Lying and False Imprisonment—*Take chicanery to the next level. This has been known to work in some civilizations, although most of those are now defunct.*

Of all of the above, the most troublesome is lying, because although we want to teach our children never to do it, we must learn to lie at the drop of a hat ourselves. When they're five years old and interrupt a coital moment, you don't want to answer the question, "What are you doing?" with, "We were having sex, dear," because the next question will invariably be, "What is sex?" and you won't want to explain that for another forty or fifty years at least (although I'll be giving it a try in Chapter 14).

BUT SERIOUSLY

THE IMPORTANT POINT IS TO USE ALL THE VARIABLES IN YOUR own personality to develop theirs. Different approaches, assorted colors and textures, varied volumes and tones, and different levels of sternness are appropriate in different situations.

Try to avoid a coddle-and-shriek household, in which the only two gears the children see are "mushy" and "pissed off." The subtleties and shadings of your own character have gotten you this far in life; give your child the benefit of your full dimension.

NAGGING QUESTIONS THAT GET YOU THINKING DEFENSIVELY

IF YOU ARE NOT RIDDLED WITH SELF-DOUBT, YOU'RE MISSING something. If you think you have all the answers, you haven't heard all the questions. Are we spending enough time with the kids? Are we singing the right songs? Are we reading the right books/watching the right TV shows? Are we being too lenient or too strict? Are they playing with the right kids? Are they going to the right schools? Is there something else we ought to know? And, finally, are we doing a good job?

Presumably, you are prepared for the physical inevitabilities and know what to do when your kid throws up/poops water/has a fever/gets a rash. But have you thought about how you'll react years from now when Mandy's ashamed of her butt and decides never to eat again, or when she wants to pierce something? What if she wants to pierce everything? And could the time come when "tough love" demands that you consider kicking your teenager out of the house? And if it does, won't you be afraid of the options, like your son peddling pot or sweet Mandy showing off in the *Girls Gone Wild* video?

Will they be Olympic champions or axe murderers? Governors and generals or circus clowns and stock cheats? (Nothing against circus clowns—it just seems like more of a part-time job.)

THAT'S OFFENSIVE

ANOTHER USEFUL FOOTBALL MAXIM STATES, "THE BEST DEFENSE is a good offense." Once you are comfortably suspicious, you may proceed with confidence that you can't be caught off guard, and that you'll use your aggressive, proactive instincts in the decisions to come.

You don't need much encouragement to cuddle and praise your child, so the balance you'll aim for will be to both teach and listen, scold and nurture, hug and nag, control and cajole.

"Cajole" may be the key, as it is, by definition, a bloodless form of negotiation: "to influence through alternately positive and negative stimuli; to prod into action without conflict," i.e., to preempt punishment.

THE LENIENCY ISSUE

MANY OF US WHO GREW UP IN THE "SPARE THE ROD, SPOIL THE child" generation came to believe that children are innately good people who, if given the option, will generally choose to do the right thing. Wrong. This is one of the planet's most dangerous misapprehensions.

Children are children for a reason: they are younger and stupider than we are. That's their job. They don't have the benefit of distance and reflection that we gained in our own tortured adolescence. A liberal democratic perspective may be good for saving caribou near the Alaska pipeline, but it doesn't work for herding kids. Parenting is a dictatorship. We are their first interpreters of the world around them, and spoiling their dangerous fun is our job.

My middle son, Robin, accused me of being too lenient and not disciplining him enough. Of course, he neglected to bring this up during the key disciplinary period of thirteen to eighteen years old, waiting until he was safely out of the house and earning his own living before pointing out my inadequacy.

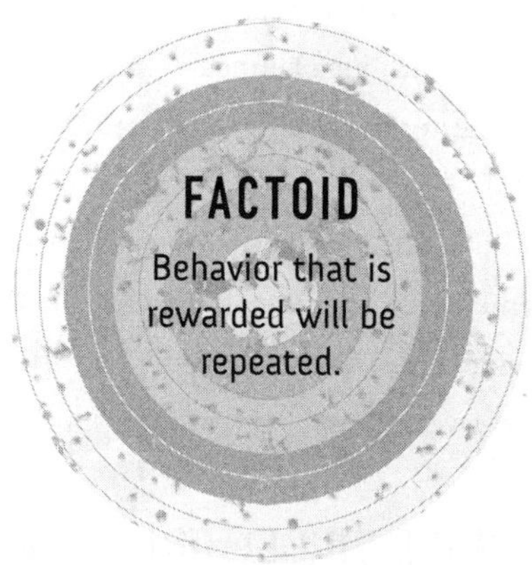

FACTOID
Behavior that is rewarded will be repeated.

MORE DUMB THINGS A PARENT COULD DO

OF ALL THE MISTAKES A PARENT COULD MAKE, I CONFESS TO being guilty of a few not-my-proudest-moment moments, some of which are too embarrassing to print (at least until the statute of limitations runs out). I'll let you guess which of the following transgressions I checked off. Maybe you'll meet my kids one day and they'll tell you whether you guessed right. Avoid the following:

a) Getting drunk with your child.

b) Helping him acquire a fake ID.

c) Letting your kid see you smoking pot.

d) Letting your kid smoke pot with you.

e) Asking him to get you some pot.

f) Hiring a lap dancer for your son's sixteenth birthday party.

g) Hiring a lap stripper for your son's eighteenth birthday party.

h) Hiring a hooker for his twenty-first birthday party.

i) Leaving your wife and kid for the stripper in point "g." (This actually happened in our neighborhood.)

j) Allowing him to have a sleepover with a friend of the opposite sex with huge breasts and few detectable morals.

k) Letting him drive without a seatbelt.

l) Letting him bike without a helmet.

m) Doing his semester book report for him.

These are the times when we look back and wonder, *What was I thinking?* Regrettably, sometimes the answer is, *Nothing.* Men have been accused of thinking with their penises, mothers of thinking with their hearts. When faced with a choice between those two, err on the side of the heart.

LIFE STORIES YOU'LL ONLY READ HERE

YOU'LL NOTICE ME REFERRING OFTEN TO MY OWN FAMILY, SO IT may be useful to include some biographical info on this beloved cast of characters. I have one young son, Carter, the age of twelve, and two grown men, Brennan and Robin, from a previous litigation. I met their mother, Gloria Loring, in Toronto when I was a fledgling writer at CBC-TV and she was already a glamorous international TV and recording star. I had seen her on Dean Martin, Carol Burnett, and Glen Campbell's shows, and when I read that she was appearing in town at the Royal

York Supper Club, I scammed a ticket and an introduction. Within six months, we were married. While I wouldn't recommend this pace for everyone, this marriage turned out to be very real, highly successful, and eminently productive—to wit, Robin and Brennan. We split when the boys were seven and nine, but despite the predictable struggles that follow divorce—community property, custody agreements, and overall bad feelings—a certain enlightened maturity informs the years that pass.

Our parenting came full circle when Robin married his high school sweetheart, the fabulous and talented actress Paula Patton (*Idlewild* with OutKast, *Déjà Vu* with Denzel—yes, that Denzel—Washington!, *Swingvote, Mirrors, Precious*). Robin invited Gloria and me to escort him down the aisle, to give away the groom in the ultimate act of joint custody: relinquishing custody. God bless him for honoring us this way and for allowing us to revel in his moment. If time doesn't heal all wounds, children certainly do.

As outspoken and theatrical as Robin has always been, Brennan has been introspective, subdued, and even shy. Brennan is consequently harder to know, but it is well worth the wait and he is invariably beloved. Those who take the time to acquaint themselves become lifelong friends, universally praising his heart and goodness. Brennan has always been unique, an individual in the truest sense who can't (or won't) work for anyone else. I never had that kind of confidence and always encouraged collaboration and general sucking up, but Brennan has proven me wrong. He has cut his own path, going from film direction to graphic arts to real estate—and he has made a mark in all three. His films were reviewed and nurtured by no less of an authority than Garry Marshall, his visual arts are on display in a permanent showcase at the Staples Center in Los Angeles, and his real estate projects are for sale in the L.A. area. If you're interested, call him. (Don't call me—dads don't get a finder's fee.)

Carter's personality seems to be a combination of the other two: he's an outgoing leader and (regrettably) an occasional class clown, but with equally intense gusts of shyness and even stage fright. It amazes me, as it will amaze you, that two or more children can be raised in identical circumstances by identical parents in identical environments, with identical rules and governing philosophies, yet have polar-opposite personalities. It is equally curious to see how two such disparate young men (Robin and Brennan) can share that unwavering, loving bond that only brothers can know.

Which brings me to my brother, Todd, producer of *America's Funniest Home Videos*, who is ten years my junior and my lifelong best friend. It was my relationship with him and my other best friend, our sister, Joanne, a Toronto chiropractor, that taught me as a teenager that one of my primary goals in life would be to have children.

It is ironic, having grown up in a highly academic family, that neither of my elder sons actually graduated from college. Robin bailed out after high school to pursue his career in the age-sensitive world of music. Brennan learned a lot in his five years of college, but skipped around enough to avoid a formal degree. I'll count on Carter's indifference to show business to assure us of some academic über-achievement in this millennium. At the age of twelve, his current passion is the National Football League, and that's okay, too, especially considering the size of those contracts.

RESPONSIBILITY

I MET CARTER'S MOTHER WHEN I HOSTED THE *MISS WORLD PAGEANT* on ABC Television and she was passing on her crown as the departing Queen of record. We hit it off, married, and had Carter five years later. A year after that, she stated her preference for separate living arrangements, and we divorced. My mother died in the middle of those proceedings. Tough year.

THE STEPMOTHER AUDITIONS

MY BOYS WERE PATIENT AND UNDERSTANDING, EVEN SYMPATHETIC, during that period of our lives known as the "Stepmother Auditions." Their counsel was always welcome and often wise. "Dump her" ... "She's after something" ... "All she wants from you is meaningless sex." That one got to stay a while.

You see, none of this child-rearing stuff flies without the love and support of your co-parent. For those of us unfortunate enough to lose a partner through death or divorce, the challenge of parenting magnifies exponentially.

For those of us lucky enough to find another partner to help with the work at hand, we must thank our stars because it's a tough job alone.

My salvation came in the form of a beautiful, sensitive, giving, caring Bolivian princess named Tanya Callau, who brightened my world one day when I was booked as the comedic entertainment for a Florida Marlins fashion show, in which she was one of the models. She was beautiful and I did what any self-respecting actor would do—I hit on her! Soon after, she was visiting L.A., and made the transition from South Beach supermodel to L.A. diaper-changer in what seemed like an instant. Carter was two at the time, and she embraced my son completely, a prerequisite for a romance like ours to prosper. Three years later, we married.

I am grateful every day for the lovely Tanya. She's the same age as my grown boys and their wives so she helps interpret them to me.

Her co-parenting of Carter all these years has made me a better father and him a finer young man. You've pulled it all together so thank you, dear Tanya—I know you'll be reading this paragraph to see how you're mentioned so I hope I've done justice to your immeasurable importance to us.

So, in reverse chronological order, I have the offspring trifecta, the hat trick: one student, one artist, and one entrepreneur, in addition to an A-list brother-sister combo and a good woman. Life is generous.

To my everlasting good fortune, it all started for me with Isadora and Willis Greer on one side and the Thickes on the other. I'll also be telling tales about the Jeffery clan, those genetic forebears to whom I owe my unyielding hairline and a treasure trove of childhood memories. I hope you like the pictures.

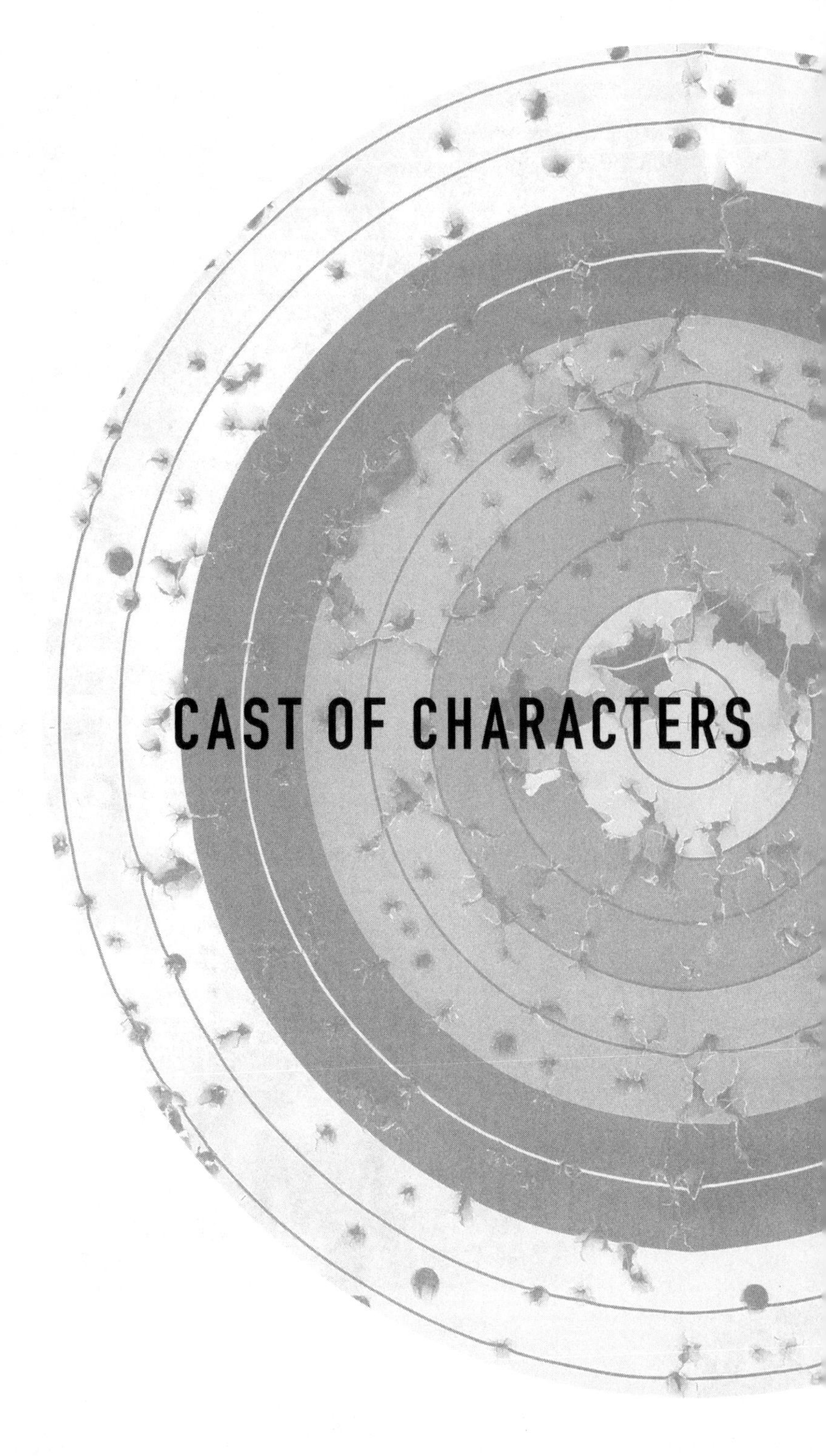

CAST OF CHARACTERS

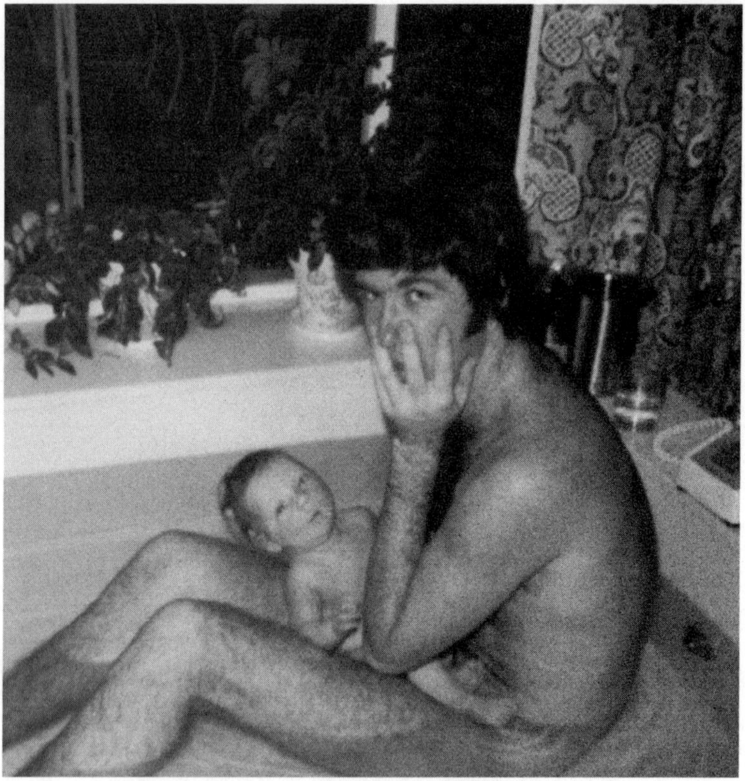

Sorry, Brennan, but every family has a picture like this

Brennan with Kanye on Line 2

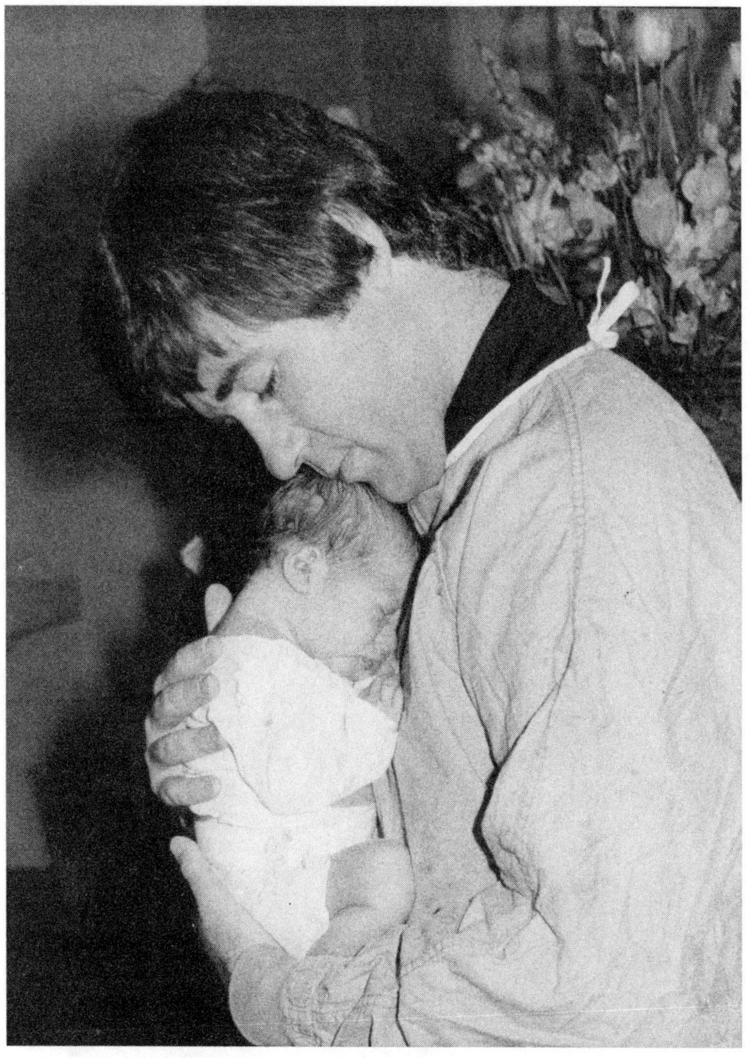

Robin, Day One

Brennan and Robin contemplate Carter's diaper

Happy Father's Day!

The same guys…airbrushed

Another proud Dad/Grandpa…Dr. Brian Thicke with Brennan and Robin

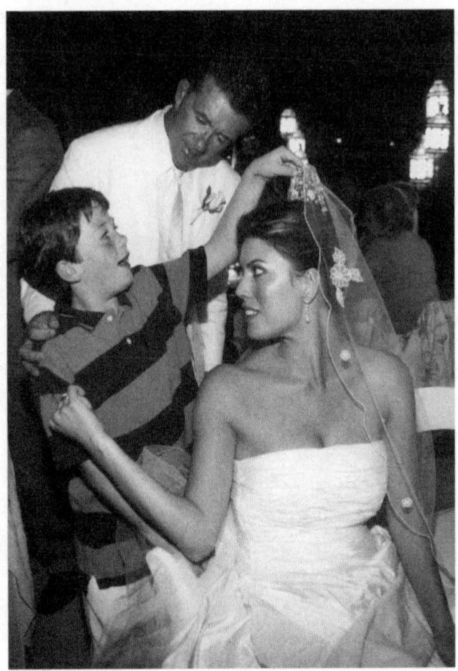

Carter-the-ring-bearer said Tanya was "pretty enough to be God's girlfriend!"

Mr. Lucky!

Joan Shirley Isabel Greer Thicke —the first woman in my life (Jan. 6, 1928–Sept. 16, 1999)

William Elgar Jeffery (Jan. 23, 1923–Feb. 16, 1999)

Isadora Sarah Brennan Greer...aka "Issie"...aka "Is" never called "Grandma"! (June 15, 1911–May 11, 2001)

Isadora and Willis Greer (Dec. 3, 1909–Aug. 17, 1992)

Is and me

Fifty years later

The Last Great Family Gathering

Surprises

Kidz in the Hood

THERE IS A PLETHORA OF ADVICE ON CHILDHOOD, PARENTHOOD, fatherhood, and motherhood, but in this age of specialization, it would be handy to learn about more specific 'hoods along the way, and there ought to be names for them. Now there are.

DIAPERHOOD—TODDLERHOOD—TANTRUMHOOD—HORMONEHOOD

AKA "ROBIN HOOD," (AFTER MY MIDDLE SON). TAKEN TOGETHER, the 'hoods are a hoot. But you'll need to pass through one to get to the next, so don't skip any or you'll never catch up.

You will recognize Diaperhood as the Age of Reaction and Toddlerhood as the Age of Discovery. Tantrumhood is the Age of Discovering How Far You Can Push Your Parents. Then, in

Hormonehood, you as an adolescent discover how far you can push the world.

If you're looking for the Age of Reason, don't bother—it doesn't exist in the parent-child dynamic of "all emotion, all the time." If you're lucky, you'll get a retrospective crack at reason when they're grown-ups.

SHAKESPEAREHOOD

NOT TO BE CRITICAL OF A COLLEAGUE, BUT THE ESTIMABLE ALL-Time Dean of English Theatre missed an opportunity in *As You Like It* to expand the 'hood dialogue. With inflation, his "Seven Ages of Man" would have grown to ten today and might have included the interim Ages of Preschool and Preteen and then Prenup for later.

JAQUES (the courtesan):
All the world's a stage,
And all the men and women merely players;
They have their exits and their entrances;
And one man in his time plays many parts,
His acts being seven ages. At first the infant,
Mewling and puking in the nurse's arms.

(There's preschool. The Shakespeares apparently had a nanny—a good thing, because in seventeenth-century England, daycare consisted of loading ten urchins in a donkey cart so Mom could churn butter at the mall. "Puking" I get, but you're on your own to define "mewling.")

Then the whining school-boy, with his satchel
And shining morning face, creeping like snail
Unwillingly to school.

("Unwillingly" would indicate Catholic school, or at least not coed. Studies show that coed classrooms have poorer grades but better attendance. Duh!)

And then the lover,
Sighing like furnace, with a woeful ballad
Made to his mistress' eyebrow.

(Hormonehood!)

Then a soldier,
Full of strange oaths, and bearded like the pard,

(I studied this play in college, but I'm not sure what a "pard" is. I could look this stuff up, but if you do it, we're interactive.)

Jealous in honor, sudden and quick in quarrel,
Seeking the bubble reputation
Even in the cannon's mouth...

(He lost me there, but that sounds like married people.)

Last scene of all,
That ends this strange eventful history,
Is second childishness and mere oblivion;
Sans teeth, sans eyes, sans taste, sans everything.

SHOCK AND AWE-FUL BEHAVIOR

TIME AND AGAIN YOUR CHILD WILL SURPRISE YOU WITH BEHAVIOR you are certain you did not exhibit at that age, but you are probably wrong and simply in denial.

Ask your parents. You were likely that ornery as a two-year-old, that clumsy as a four-year-old, just as reckless at eight, and quite impossible at fifteen. Be aware—not naïve—and make each Age better than the last.

Firsts

Virgin Territory

IF THIS IS YOUR FIRST CHILD, YOU'VE JUST SURVIVED YOUR FIRST pregnancy—which was enriched, it is hoped, by reading *How Men Have Babies: The Pregnant Father's Survival Guide*. As an addendum to the advice in that work, I have one more important lesson that men must carry from Pregnanthood through to Parenthood. That is, *Be a Man*.

If there is ever a time to put "gender equality" on hiatus, it's while a woman is expecting. Never will it be more obvious that there is, indeed, a difference between the sexes than while she's barfing and you're watching football, or when she's writhing in labor while your big chore is remembering to say, "Breathe!"

Be a Man in every way you've ever heard about: be wise, be patient, be nurturing, be sensitive. But mostly, be strong, be a rock, be a tower—the one she can count on when her world is spinning out of control. Let her be vulnerable and uncertain while you are John Wayne, Jackie

Chan, or whatever Super Hero comes to mind as the prototypical ass-kicker she'll need by her side.

A FIRST TIME FOR EVERYTHING

YOU'LL FEEL THE LOVE AS YOU NOTE HIS FIRST WORD, FIRST STEP, first song, first movie or TV favorite, and you'll fondly remember his first playdate, his first joke, his first pet—followed by his first dead pet. (My sister got a live rabbit for Easter and loved it to death. Literally. After much excitement and hugging and cuddling, the Easter bunny was found to be curiously immobile. Oops!) Be prepared to explain the whole *Lion King* "Circle of Life" thing when he or she discovers the Discovery Channel ("Everybody has to eat!").

NEVER TRY TO BAPTIZE A CAT

Another pet hazard safety tip.

Along those lines, your baby's first swimming lesson will be important, as this skill is key for his safety and your peace of mind. Try tossing him in the pool as early as six months—it may work, really!

BABY'S FIRST PRAYER...

Will be much simpler than your laundry list of items requiring divine intervention.

You'll wonder at his first questions about God and you'll fret about his first skinned knee, bee sting, and flu shot.

Who will his first friends be?

You'll never forget his first day of school, and you'll elbow your way to the front row with your handicam to tape his first recital. ("Is he the angel or the tree?")

Your refrigerator will hold more art than milk, and you'll laminate his first report card.

You'll cringe at the first bad word he brings home from the bad kids.

How did you react to his first fight? Were you impressed or did you scold him? Was he hurt and were you worried?

Did you teach him the value of a dollar when you gave him his first allowance? Did you catch yourself saying, "When I was your age I only got..."?

The first time he was rejected by a girl, did you:

a) Call and berate her parents?

b) Distract him with a new dog?

c) Remind him she's ugly?

d) Remind him he's ugly?

How did you handle his disappointment when he heard the whole Santa industry might be based on a myth?

Have you thought about the role you'll play in his first employment, first driving lesson, first car, first credit card, and first loan?

WHY YOU MIGHT WANT TO SKIP A FEW CHAPTERS

REMINDER: HERE COME THE PARTS THAT DEAL MOSTLY WITH infants, so if you've already raised/alienated a toddler, feel free to go to Chapter 7, although you do so at the risk of missing references to Bobby Orr, nipples, violence, sex (the early years), and Jessica Simpson. Your call. On the other hand, you might want to test yourself on how you did in those start-up stages. Still your call.

A THRILL A MINUTE

MOST OF THE FIRSTS WILL BE DELIGHTFUL FOR YOU AND YOUR mate, and handled properly these milestones will become the memories that define your very lives. In addition to the thrilling list above, there will be many more surprises:

FIRST GLIMPSE: "THAT PRUNE CAN'T BE MY KID!"

"There is only one pretty child in the world, and every mother has it."

– Narcissistic proverb

At the moment of birth, you may be rendered speechless. If you could talk, it might be to say, "There must be some mistake!" A word of caution to the husband: do the right thing from birth or you'll never forgive yourself. Worse yet, neither will the missus. That is to say, when you first see the baby, don't act all disappointed because she looks like a prop from *War of the Worlds*. Your baby will not likely notice that you'd rather have a new putter than this wrinkled sausage, but your wife will note your letdown—as she will every detail of this birthday—and if you've made a misstep, you will pay for the rest of your days. Wives keep a log of all the bad things you've ever done or said on computer chips in their heads, saving such trivia to throw at you during a vulnerable moment four years down the road, long after such memories have been purged from your own databanks. Get on board with Mom at the get-go and plan to stay there at all costs.

WHO PAINTED HIM BLUE?

It's not unusual for the baby to come out bluish, so don't panic. When circulatory and respiratory systems kick in, you'll see a color you can relate to.

Some babies are born covered with a white coating called "vernix," which gives the baby a ruddy appearance. The nurse will clean away most of the vernix, and what remains is likely to peel away shortly after birth. It can look like peeling skin after a sunburn, but they're just dead cells, and the child will feel no pain. (You'll find this kind of useful knowledge in *The New Father's Panic Book* by Gene B. Williams, Avon Books.)

Most babies have wrinkled skin, but before you consider Botox, know that "wrinkled" is normal and goes away quickly.

Be patient at the hospital, and odds are your baby will look better by the time you get him home.

WHO PAINTED HIM YELLOW?

Mild jaundice is not uncommon, because the newborn's liver may not be mature enough to dispel an orange-tinted pigment the body produces, called bilirubin. Usually all the baby needs is a few minutes of sunlight on his skin each day to break down the pigment. Some indirect sunlight is good, but you're not grooming a Hawaiian Tropic model here, so be sure your child isn't exposed to strong direct sunlight.

Frequent nursing and additional water may also offer relief. Monitor this condition to make sure it's not a symptom of infection or other medical conditions.

Another visual exam will be for birthmarks (hemangiomas).

The genital area is often swollen, which can be a source of great pride in the father of a boy child, but don't get all cocky—no pun intended—because this, too, shall pass.

CIRCUMCISION

Get this wrong and nothing else will matter, ever!

You don't get a second shot here, so put your son's future in the hands of a professional. The penis will be red and sore for a few days after the circumcision. Hopefully, you paid full price and didn't have it done at Benihana's, but mere redness and soreness is not a bad thing. You'll need to protect the newly exposed tip and keep it from sticking to the inside of the diaper. It is perfectly normal to see a few tiny spots of blood on his diaper for a few days, but keep the unit dry and that tip lubricated with petroleum jelly, and wrap it in gauze to protect it from irritation due to contact with urine.

Years later, if you can also teach him how to handle rejection in matters related to this instrument, you've done all that can be expected.

CAN YOU HEAR ME NOW?

Within hours of the actual birth, you'll be on the phone. Who did you call first:

a) Your parents?
b) Her parents?
c) Wolf Blitzer?
d) The President?

I called Bobby Orr when my first was born. Yes, that Bobby Orr—the Boston Bruin. He was a pal and had called me when his first was born a few months earlier. I remember the honor I felt, and you, too, will have the opportunity to share your joy at that historic moment with a select list of friends and relatives, so think about it beforehand. Your kid will be impressed to hear you know someone famous. Let's hope you're in solid with Jon and Kate by now.

FIRST POOP AND BEYOND

NOW HE'S HOME AND THE PRESSURE'S ON.

He should urinate about twenty-four hours after the birth and then as many as eighteen times every twenty-four hours, a schedule a woman will maintain for life.

In two days, he should have his first bowel movement, and then he'll have about five a day for the following weeks. The material passed shortly after birth is called meconium. It looks like dark green tar and has little or no odor. Enjoy that while it lasts, because everything after this will stink to high heaven.

He probably won't eat much for the first twenty-four hours, after which he'll want seven to eight feedings a day, because his metabolism will be twice as fast as yours.

REFLEXES

A healthy baby will react to the world around him. If you touch his cheek, he will turn in search of food. This rooting reflex is actually a nipple search and will disappear in boys around age eighty.

The sucking reflex will cause the baby to begin sucking even if all he has found is your finger.

When the Moro reflex kicks in, the baby's arms and legs tighten, most commonly as a reaction to a loud noise, such as a clap.

If you touch the baby's palm, he will close his fingers in the grasping reflex. At age sixteen, the reflex returns—at the sight of your wallet.

THE EYES HAVE IT

In those first days, he'll be able to focus his eyes for a few seconds on an object ten inches from his face. If you are the first face he sees, at least have the decency to shave, and make sure there's nothing sticking out of your nose or teeth. Don't worry if your baby looks back at you cross-eyed or uses just one eye while the other drifts. This is something he does on purpose to frighten you. Play games that stimulate and exercise the baby's eyes.

FIRST LEAKY NIPPLE

A girl or boy may have a leaking of milk from the nipples, caused by hormones from the mother in the baby's system.

More shocking to some parents is the possibility that a newborn girl will have what seems to be a period. Any bleeding should always be checked by a doctor, but this is most often not a concern.

Your baby's umbilical cord stump will drop off one or two weeks after he's born. Meanwhile, limit your baby washing to sponge baths. Keep the stump as dry as possible and clean it with rubbing alcohol every time you change his diaper. Folding down the front of the diaper exposes the stump to more air and speeds up the falling-off process.

FIRST BATH

Some babies find warm water soothing while others freak out when they get wet. If you try bathing a crying infant, don't do it alone. Holding onto a calm soapy baby is tough enough, but maintaining a grip on a squirming, screaming slippery one takes a team of highly trained professionals. Afterwards, towel the baby briskly to stimulate the skin. Remember, always support the neck and head while picking up a newborn.

FIRST RECTAL INVASION

Taking a baby's temperature by holding a thermometer under his tongue is not practical or safe. Temperature readings taken through the anus are more accurate, but they are unpleasant for the baby and no walk in the park for the parent. Get his mom to perform this task because it's possible you will never be forgiven for this intrusion. Most pediatricians are satisfied with the accuracy of the thermometer-in-the-armpit method.

MEWLING OR PUKING?

His first illness may not be an illness at all, unless you consider your own paranoia to be life-threatening. Admit it, you assume the worst with any symptom. Your pediatrician expects you to be a pain in the ass, so why not avail yourself of the high-tech diagnostic tools available to monitor your child's health? You'll learn soon enough to distinguish between real and imagined illnesses, but in the meantime, take the "better safe than sorry" route and keep the number of visitors to a minimum in his first month home to avoid germs. No runny noses need apply.

DIAPER RASH

Your baby's bottom requires good air circulation, so don't use rubber or plastic pants with cloth diapers. When the rash shows up, let your baby frolic for a few minutes without a diaper, but make sure it's on a towel or old blanket you don't ever care to use again. Apply some diaper cream with each change.

Boudreaux's Butt Paste is a diaper rash cream, a mixture of zinc oxide, castor oil, mineral oil, boric acid, and Peruvian balsam. Mr. Boudreaux also recommends his Butt Paste for acne, chapped lips, poison ivy, and jock itch. Go figure. This product became popular with athletes at Louisiana State University, where they go through about fifteen pounds a year, according to athletic trainer Jack Marucci. Jack also enthuses that Butt Paste "keeps the chafing at bay." Catchy slogan.

FIRST PIMPLES

These are usually confined to the baby's face, another result of the wife's hormones continuing to swim through the baby's system, or of the baby's underdeveloped pores. Either way, don't squeeze, pick at, or scrub these pimples. Just wash them gently with water several times a day, pat them dry, and they'll go away in a few months. On the other hand, your child may simply be a pimply-faced geek for life, but let's not obsess yet. About *this*, anyway.

CRADLE CAP (SEBORRHEIC DERMATITIS)

Now you know I've done my research. How else would I know a term like that? This looks like a flaky, yellowish, sometimes greasy dandruff that usually shows up on the scalp but can also work its way into the baby's eyebrows. Frequent shampooing with baby shampoo should get rid of it. Otherwise, just chalk it up as your baby's first bad hair day and go back to worrying about those pimples.

FRANKINCENSE AND MYRRH

Don't use any kind of scented products like powder, lotions, or even diaper wipes, because bugs love them. Until the age of six months, don't use any sunscreen on your baby, because it's filled with chemicals that can trigger allergic reactions. Wear clothes that are fun to snuggle, because kids hate scratchy things.

CRYBABIES

No matter how well you've handled all of the above, your kid will cry. Don't take it personally. This does not reflect your total failure as a human being. Sometimes it's OK to let the baby "cry it out," but generally speaking, you should respond promptly and lovingly to your baby's tears. If the crying goes on for more than twenty minutes, you might put the baby in his crib and give yourself a break. If the baby is still screaming after another ten minutes, pick him up and try the whole process again. If he's still crying after an hour, move away without leaving a forwarding address, or pester that pediatrician again.

FIRST TEETH

Your baby's teeth started forming when your wife was four months pregnant, although they won't make their first appearance (eruption, in dental language) until age six or seven months. When they arrive they'll be followed immediately by plaque, the same stuff your dentist has to chip off your teeth with a chisel. Use a small piece of gauze to clean his teeth once a day. When he's a year old, use a toothbrush with soft bristles. The first teeth you'll see will be the two lower central incisors, and most kids will have all eight incisors by the end of their first year. Expect some discomfort around the tooth for a few days before it breaks through the gum, days marked by a runny nose, loose stools, low-grade fever, and general crankiness. Try acetaminophen—your pediatrician will tell you how many drops to give—and don't waste your time rubbing it on the baby's gums, because that doesn't work. Teething rings can do the trick, especially the kind that are water filled and freezable. You can also try frozen bagels—the cold is soothing.

FIRST SNEEZE

Kids who received antibiotics, such as penicillin, in their first six months are more likely to develop allergies and asthma than kids who didn't get the drugs; the suspicion being that these drugs interfere with the development of the immune system. Asthma and food allergies are less common in children who were breast fed for more than four months.

FIRST NEEDLES

Are vaccines themselves dangerous? Are the risks worth the rewards? Do I look like a freakin' doctor? Your pediatrician will help you decide among shots for diphtheria, pertussis (whooping cough), tetanus, polio, measles, rubella (German measles), typhus, meningitis, pneumonia, spotted fever, measles, mumps, and chicken pox. Most schools require proof of vaccination before you enroll your child.

REALITY TV IN YOUR HOUSE

YOU HAVE ALREADY BEEN VIDEO RECORDING YOUR CHILD'S first...everything, because his inaugural experiences are momentous in world history, right up there with the sinking of the Titanic, the fall of the Berlin Wall, and where were you when you heard about LeAnn Rimes and that studly Eddie guy?

This will be the most documented generation of all time, and your kid will be his own twenty-four-hour reality show, his life saved, downloaded, e-mailed, printed, copied, sent as an attachment, and instant messaged to the entire known universe.

As a child, I was neglected on film, because the state of the video art was primitive and apparently my dad was waiting for the price of cameras to go down. It took the birth of a sister ten years later to get my parents up to speed. By the time my brother, Todd, arrived, we all but had a live-in camera crew. (It is fitting that Todd later went on to produce *America's Funniest Home Videos*!) Psychologists tell us we treat our firstborns differently from our second and third kids, so don't feel guilty if you're over it by kid number four and find yourself hoping he will just draw a lot of pictures of himself.

WHY ORAL IS GOOD

Relax, it's not what you're thinking. Oral history is an art form that must not be lost in the easy-to-document world of video technology. What "firsts" do you remember about your childhood? What are your earliest memories of people and places? As your child grows and you impart your values and life lessons, it will be impossible to avoid the "when I was your age" form of storytelling, nor should you, so be sure your stories are interesting and well told.

WHO IS THIS DORK?

Your folks probably taught that you only get one chance to make a first impression, and your baby's first impression of anything will likely be the one you give him. Every act, every decision, could have permanent consequences. So don't blow it.

FACTOID

Families with pets during the child's first year see a lower incidence of allergies and asthma.

Nutrition

How to Feed Kids Who Won't Hate You

WHEN THEY REFUSE TO EAT, DO YOU:

a) Eat their portions instead?
b) Feed them intravenously?
c) Cover the pork chops in sugar?

Letting them eat whatever they want will require very little cooking and mostly involves opening a box of frosted cereal or PopTarts. This is followed by a burst of excitement, which is followed in turn by a glazed-over, glassy-eyed look and the inability to hear or follow any further instruction. Repeat every mealtime until the kid is lethargic, overweight, and in danger of developing serious lifelong health problems.

GAG ME WITH A SPOON

INFANTS WILL EAT WHEN THEY'RE HUNGRY, TODDLERS WILL EAT at mealtimes, and children will be finicky. Nutrition is important, but meals should be pleasant and positive highlights of the day. Don't turn supper into a tortured tug-of-war by making them eat peas if they're dead set against it for whatever reason, including simple stubbornness.

"Because they're good for you" is a tough concept to sell a kid who's mewling or puking. And why doesn't anybody say "supper" anymore? Why is it always "dinner" when "supper" has such a warm feel?

Your child will have individual tastes in music, clothes, friends, and, yes, food. Where does it say he has to like everything or even try everything?

EATING WITH A SPOON

IT'S HARD TO REMEMBER WHEN WE WERE THIS USELESS. SPOON competence is one of the things adults take for granted. When your baby starts regarding utensils as more than weapons, be sure he has acquired the skill and dexterity to use them. Don't protest if he's left-handed, but do make him hold a spoon as he will a pencil, because learning one grip for both will simplify his life forever.

SMALLER BITES

PRESENT KIDS WITH MODEST PORTIONS AND YOU'LL REDUCE the likelihood of them overeating. Children themselves are the best judges of how much food they need, according to Jennifer Fisher, assistant professor of pediatrics at Baylor College of Medicine in Houston.

WHO'S YOUR (SUGAR) DADDY?

CANDY GORGING—THE KIND YOU SEE ON SACRED HOLIDAYS LIKE Halloween—can cause indigestion or worse: gastroesophageal reflux disease, or GERD.

Known to adults as heartburn, this disorder can strike children who eat large quantities of chocolate, peppermint, or spearmint candies, which tend to open up the valve between the esophagus and the stomach and allow acid to pass back into the food pipe. If left untreated, GERD can lead to complications, including difficulty swallowing, pneumonia, and eventually esophageal cancer. Telltale signs include vomiting, inability to sleep, complaints of a persistent sour taste in the mouth, bad breath, chronic coughing, pain after lying down, or a hoarse voice upon waking up.

Elevating the head of the bed and having the child lie on his left side at night, which tips the stomach so that gravity can hold the acid down, can relieve GERD. Kids should cut down on soda and citrus products, stay away from secondhand smoke, and avoid pants or skirts with tight waistbands.

Don't try antacids without checking with your pediatrician.

I bet you never thought you'd someday know so much about a thing called GERD. You're now a GERD nerd.

FOOD RULES

BY NOW, WE'VE AGREED THAT "NO RULES" GUARANTEES "NO conflict." Having no food rules further assures you of parenting a puffy, sluggish oaf. Ignore the following at your mutual peril:

- Low-fat products are not necessarily low in calories.
- Juice has more calories and less fiber than the fruit it comes from.
- Oil and vinegar dressing is packed with calories but contains lots

of heart-healthy monounsaturated fatty acids. I don't know what monounsaturated fatty acids are, and I don't care as much as I should.

- If there are two types of cookies on a plate, the temptation is to eat one of each. The fewer our choices, the less we eat.
- To know how many calories you need in a day, the American Heart Association's rule of thumb is to multiply your weight in pounds by thirteen. (If you want to lose weight, subtract 250 calories.)
- All things being equal, fat people use more soap.
- Meat has been a great source of protein and vitamins since prehistoric times, and many anthropologists credit meat with playing a key role in the evolution of our species (the development of hunting skills comes to mind). One leg of mammoth contains many more calories than raw roots and berries, meaning that prehistoric man didn't have to eat all day to get the nutrition he needed. That freed him up to pursue intellectual activity such as cave painting and storytelling.

Nowadays, we eat roughly twice as much protein as we need, putting a strain on our kidneys and livers.

BAD NEWS

FATS HAVE MORE FLAVOR. MORE ACCURATELY, FATS ENHANCE flavor. Vegetarians may risk becoming iron-deficient, which can lead to anemia. I'm a semi-vegetarian now—I only eat animals that eat vegetables.

Broccoli, Brussels sprouts, and green beans are good for you. Potatoes, on the other hand, are useless. OK, maybe they have vitamin B, copper, potassium, and calcium, but a potato's main act is to thicken soup. Big deal.

You can eat a lot of kidney beans, lentils, and chickpeas. They're low in fat and calories and packed with fiber, protein, and minerals—and they fill you up.

Nuts and seeds make up a major part of the diet in some cultures. They're high in calories, protein, and key nutrients, especially vitamin E.

According to a preliminary study, a diet high in vitamin E decreases the risk of developing Alzheimer's. If you forget this, it's already too late.

Seafood is not perfect. Oily fish can carry toxins, and swordfish, shark, and mackerel can have altogether too much mercury, although I suspect it's only worrisome if you eat about a shark a day.

Salmon—both farmed and wild—can contain high levels of PCBs (polychlorinated biphenyls), and species from polluted waters should never be eaten under any circumstances. (If salmonella comes from chickens, why doesn't chickenella come from salmon?)

CHICKEN SHTICK

EGGS GIVE YOU PROTEIN, NUTRIENTS, AND VITAMINS—PROBABLY the best bargain in the grocery store—but eggs have twice the cholesterol of beef, so three or four a week are plenty.

FROOT LOOP FOLLIES

I ALWAYS WRITE SOMETHING ABOUT DIABETES BECAUSE MY ELDEST, Brennan, was diagnosed with the disease at age four. I'm sure you'd do the same—in fact, his mom, Gloria Loring, has written an entire book about it: *Parenting a Child with Diabetes* (McGraw-Hill).

This disease affects one in ten children, and new info suggests you can cut your baby's odds of getting type 1 diabetes by sticking to the recommended schedule of introducing cereals at four to six months—any earlier or later and the onset of the disease is more likely.

EAT IT OR BEAT IT: YOUR FACTOID FOOD QUIZ

HOW MUCH OF EACH TYPE OF FOOD DOES THE AVERAGE ADULT American eat in a year?

- Lettuce: 25 lbs. Tomatoes: 92 lbs. (Mostly processed, as in ketchup or pasta sauce.) French fries: 51 lbs. Potato chips: 17 lbs.
- Every second, 127 chickens get eaten in America.
- Americans eat 2 billion hot dogs every year.
- A kid will have eaten 1,500 peanut butter and jelly sandwiches by the time he graduates from high school. Americans consume 700 million pounds of peanut butter each year! (That's enough to cover the floor of the Grand Canyon, although there seems to be no environmentally sound reason to do so.)
- According to the Kaiser Family Foundation, kids watch 40,000 TV ads per year—many of them for cereals, candy, and fast food—compared to 20,000 in the '70s. Obese kids generally watch more TV and are no doubt tempted by the food ads.
- 30 percent of American girls age nine to fourteen are on diets. 16 percent of boys in that age group are on diets. Kids who diet frequently, however, are found to gain two to three pounds more each year than their peers who do not diet. The likely reason is overly restrictive diets that lead to cycles of binge eating.

Safety

Home Sweet Homeland Security

CLEAR AND PRESENT DANGER

DON'T EXPECT THE TYKES TO THANK YOU FOR IT, BUT THE comfort and safety you provide are at the core of the love they feel for you.

You must childproof your house. Get down on your hands and knees, crawl around from the baby's perspective, and search for those Weapons of Mass Destruction—and do it more than once, because you're going to miss something. If your baby swallows something, don't put your finger blindly into the baby's mouth. That might push the object in deeper and make the choking worse or damage tender throat tissues. Learn CPR ASAP. Your pediatrician or hospital will have references for classes or instructors who will come to your house and teach basic first aid.

HEY, BUBBLE BOY

YOU WILL WANT TO PROTECT HIM FROM GERMS, BUT EVERYDAY exposure will build immunities. However, keep him away from his sniffling cousin, the uncle who likes to smell "natural," and that neighbor who always seemed to have a rat.

STRANGER ANXIETY

FEAR OF STRANGERS PEAKS AT AROUND NINE TO TEN MONTHS, but babies who have received nurturing care from a variety of familiar people—mother, father, siblings, grandparents, and a regular babysitter—seem less likely to fear strangers than babies whose only experience is with parents.

When parental leave is up and it's time to venture back to the real world, let the baby get used to a new caregiver over the course of a weekend or several evenings for short periods at a time. If this doesn't work, plan to stay home forever. If you're a parent who works long hours, your baby may perceive you as somewhat of an outsider and cling to your spouse instead of going to you; this is not necessarily a sign of your spouse's superior parenting skills (or your inferior ones), but merely a reminder that you haven't been around enough. Try rising a little earlier to take on those morning baby chores, and the whole family will love you for it.

QUIZ FOR BABYSITTERS

WHAT NUMBER DO YOU DIAL FOR 911? THAT WAS A TRICK QUESTION, but if your sitter gets it wrong, you've got the wrong sitter.

Make sure the sitter has the details on her own whereabouts as well as yours. Your address should be at her fingertips, as well as main intersections, the baby's doctor and relatives, and a map to the nearest hospital. Provide authorization/permission for emergency medical procedures.

The best sitter is someone your baby is already familiar with, but don't wait until the last minute to look for help.

SIBLING SITTERS

ON MY WATCH, MY KID BROTHER, AT AGE SEVEN, DID A DUMB thing. He threw a boomerang to see if it would come back, and then he just stood there. It came back. I got Dad, and the two of us took Todd to the hospital, where he received six stitches. As the older brother, I was obliged to remind him to duck. Sorry, Todd, but that scar gives you character.

AU PAIR

THAT'S FRENCH FOR "GIRL YOUR WIFE WILL INSTINCTIVELY HATE." *Au pairs* are usually young women who come to the States in a year-long cultural exchange administered by the United States Information Agency. There are eight USIA-approved placement agencies—use any other agency and she could be subject to immediate deportation, and you to a $10,000 fine.

The *au pair*'s purpose is to care for your children (and to pose a constant threat to your wife, who will suspect that the child in you will ultimately go to pieces in the presence of a twenty-two-year-old Swedish girl's impeccable bone structure). With any luck, your *au pair* will not be languishing at the mall with her new American friends or hitting on your teenage son from a previous marriage. On the plus side, *au pairs* are exempt from social security, Medicare, and unemployment taxes, while they provide up to forty-five hours a week of live-in child care. They can stay only one year, for which you can expect to pay around $12,000 for salary, airfare, insurance, educational allowances, room and board, and additional household expenses—marital counselors and attorneys not included.

THINGS TO ASK YOUR *AU PAIR*

CAREFUL NOW.

a) What previous childcare experience have you had?

b) Can you tell us about your own childhood?

c) Do you know infant CPR?

d) Would you spank a child?

e) Is that a thong?

f) Do you speak English? Are you understanding any of this?

g) What are your favorite things to do with kids? (This will tell you a lot.)

GOOD TOY, BAD TOY

SAFE TOYS INCLUDE BLOCKS, SHOES, MUSIC MAKERS, BALLS, dolls, and household items with various textures. Unsafe toys include anything small enough to swallow, anything made with foam, or anything that could pinch the baby—a live lobster would be a bad toy, for instance. Also avoid anything that runs on electricity. Toys with strings, ribbons, buttons, and elastic bands are all potential choking hazards.

FOREARMED IS FOREWARNED

DO YOU REMEMBER SAYING, "IF YOU TOUCH THAT REMOTE control/vase/necklace/stove, I'll break your arm"? Apparently, some of you did. A study in the *Journal of the American Medical Association* found that forearm fractures among girls and boys eight to fourteen have almost doubled in the past thirty years.

NOT IN YOUR HOME, BUT...

FOR THIRTY YEARS, THE CHILDREN'S DEFENSE FUND HAS BEEN a strong, effective voice for the children of America who cannot vote, lobby, or speak for themselves. According to the organization's founder, Marian Wright Edelman, campaigns by the CDF to prevent teen pregnancy have seen birth rates drop by 10 percent for all teens.

Gun deaths of children are down almost 50 percent since 1994, but Ms. Edelman cautions that there is still much work to be done for child advocacy. On average, a child is abused every thirty-six seconds, a teen mother gives birth about every minute, and a youth is killed by gunfire every three hours. Shocking.

EXCERPTS FROM "WHAT CHILDREN SHOULD BE TAUGHT"

THE NATIONAL CENTER FOR MISSING AND EXPLOITED CHILDREN offers important guidelines. Teach your children these points, and repeat them several times, because one mention at age five won't stick:

- Do not get into a car or go anywhere with any person unless your parents have told you that it is OK.
- Do not talk to grown-ups and others who say they need your assistance. (E.g., "Your mother is in trouble and I will take you to her.") They should not be asking children for help—they should be asking older people.
- If someone makes you nervous, asks you to do anything that makes you uncomfortable, or scares you, tell your parents or a teacher or another trusted adult. No one should approach you or touch you in a way that makes you feel uncomfortable. If someone does, tell a parent immediately.

Be alert to a teenager or adult who is paying an unusual amount of attention to your children or giving them inappropriate gifts. For more, see http://www.missingkids.com.

SLEEPING TOGETHER

NO, NOT WITH THE *AU PAIR*. GO AHEAD AND SLEEP WITH YOUR baby, because he'll be too big one day. Just don't roll over.

Put the baby against the wall or between the parents, trim your toenails, and don't drink or take medication that might make you hard to wake up.

After the first year, establish a schedule for those sleepovers so that the child recognizes a pattern, such as every other night or once a week. Over the years, that schedule will become weekends only or special occasions, such as birthdays and Christmas Eve. Do not open yourself up to a potential "negotiation" as soon as your kid is bright enough to start campaigning for the pleasure of your overnight company every bedtime.

How late in life can they sleep with you? Psychologist Dr. George Patterson (www.drgeorgep.com) says this:

"When the newborn is ready to be nursed, it is often more convenient to do it in the parents' bed. Later, a parent might feel anguish when you hear the sobbing child, and guilt over the suffering you believe you've created by 'abandoning' him and forcing him to sleep alone. The obstacle is hurdled in a week if Mom and Dad stick to their guns and give reassurance without giving in. Kids by the age of two should be sleeping regularly in their own bed, with exceptions for unusual circumstances and special occasions. The costs of delaying the transition are intimacy loss for the parents and power shift to the child (who learns he or she can control you with tears and screaming). Give your child the opportunity to 'self-soothe' and not be so dependent."

Ultimately, it's a personal choice, but if your son still wants to sleep with Mom and Dad when he brings his girlfriend home, not even Dr. Patterson can help you.

FACTOID

Grandmothers who provide childcare for nine hours or more a week have a 55 percent higher risk of having a heart attack than grandmothers who pretend to be busy and keep their babysitting to a minimum (according to a survey of 55,000 registered nurses).

Playtime

"If You Fall and Break Your Leg, Don't Come Running to Me!"

ARE WE HAVING FUN YET?

MORE THAN YOU EVER IMAGINED. IF YOU'VE BEEN PAYING PROPER attention to your child, you have never felt so important. This Mom-and-Dad thing is a blast, and by age one the fun is interactive and brings out the child in you. But be careful that it's the smart, responsible child in you and not the dolt who played with sharp objects and set his 'jammies on fire. Much about your child is developed through play, so get down on the floor and enjoy!

TOUCHING MOMENTS

THE NEW FATHER, BY ARMIN BROTT, HAS RECOMMENDATIONS

for developing tactile awareness: "Let your baby play with a small toy without letting her see it. You might want to do this in the dark or with her hands in a paper bag." (Does this sound like something they would teach at a very cruel daycare center?) Mr. Brott suggests that you "put that toy in a bag with several other toys she's never played with." (This torture has been going on for a while.) "Many babies this age will pick up the familiar toy." (The point is that you're encouraging baby to use the two faculties of touch and memory simultaneously, and that's a good idea.) Mr. Brott continues, "If your baby isn't ready for this one, don't worry, just try it again in a few weeks." (Yes, if she hasn't crawled away from home.)

MASSEUSE, MONSIEUR

IF THE BABY IS A NERVOUS WRECK FROM THE PRESSURE OF trying to pick the right toy, a massage may be just the answer. Start the massage when the baby is calm—when he's played with a toy that hasn't punctured or strangled him. Use baby oil or lotion and a combination of straight and circular strokes. Keep the pressure gentle but firm. Babies don't like a very light touch, which they perceive as tickling.

Seriously, now, thanks, Mr. Brott, for some cool ideas, and I hope you don't mind me pulling your leg—hey, there's another menacing move you can try on your kid. Other helpful books by Mr. Brott include *Throwaway Dads* (Houghton Mifflin) and *The Single Father: A Dad's Guide to Parenting without a Partner* (Abbeville Press).

READING

READ HIM ANYTHING YOU WANT. YOUR BABY DOESN'T KNOW what you're talking about anyway. The point here is to get your child accustomed to the rhythm and sound of your voice. Book time should be a peaceful, secure interlude in his otherwise hectic day. Check out Jim Trelease's *The Read-Aloud Handbook* (Penguin) and gather your favorite stories to share.

MUSIC AND SELF

YOUR CHILD HAS TO TRUST YOUR JUDGMENT ABOUT HIM AND know that your assessments are not colored by some blinding parental bias, whether it's his refrigerator art, accordion lessons, or dance classes. By school age, he knows when he stinks at something, and your opinion will become suspect if you aren't at least guardedly honest about how lousy he plays the violin. If the point of childhood activities is effort, enjoyment, and team play, the kids don't have to be good, just punctual. Tell them to show up, do their best, and have a good time, and your kids will appreciate your semi-candid reviews.

LEARN A SONG YOU WON'T MIND SINGING A MILLION TIMES

YOUR CHILD, LIKE ANY AUDIENCE, WILL DEMAND HIS FAVORITE. Over and over.

One song will do. There are CDs available of professionals singing every type of kid's song imaginable, and that can take the pressure off you to get things started. If you're not confident about your own singing, be sure to get a CD of seasonal songs and Christmas carols as sung by real singers, because you want the holidays to be full of good memories for the little ones.

I was delighted that Carter's kindergarten curriculum included traditional folk songs. Let's not lose sight of "She'll Be Comin' 'Round the Mountain," "Shenandoah," and "Jimmy Crack Corn" just because they want to hear 50 Cent and Nelly in the car. (No, "Jimmy Crack Corn" is not a drug you'll have to worry about them smoking.)

I made a list of sentimental favorites from my childhood and burned a CD—legally—to pass on to Carter, including "Thumbelina," "76 Trombones," "Teddy Bear's Picnic," "Tie Me Kangaroo Down," and "Pink Cadillac." OK, they weren't all folk favorites. What are yours?

THE RHYTHM METHOD

YOU'LL NOTICE THAT YOUR BABY ALREADY HAS A RUDIMENTARY sense of rhythm. Lay him on the floor and turn on the stereo, and he will move his arms and legs, not in time to the music, but in response to it. Try different types of music, from showtunes to hip-hop. There is no documented advantage to hearing rap at any age, but maybe those study results just aren't in yet. If Eminem had grown up listening to his own stuff, who knows? He might have turned out angry or violent. (I hear he's mellowed now.)

AUTO-IMMUNITY

CAR TRIPS CAN EITHER BE A FUN FAMILY OUTING OR A highway to hell.

Car travel tends to knock babies out and can screw up their sleep schedule, so try to leave an hour before your baby's usual nap time so that once he falls asleep, you can get as far as possible without having to amuse him. Mr. Brott advises stopping at interesting places to pet the cows, watch road repair crews, and point out forests. This is especially challenging in urban areas, where you might need to train your child to duck at the sound of gunfire. He also recommends going to an automatic car wash, which can be a thrill for some kids. I'd like to meet this Mr. Brott.

Good things to bring along on car trips include food, drinks, and books. If your car is old and you plan to drive it into the ground, you could also bring stickers, crayons, and marking pens because few buyers will be interested in your child's Sharpie artwork on the upholstery.

Never leave your child alone in the car, because babies can suffocate faster than you can imagine. If you're smart enough to be reading this book, I'll assume you already knew this. Otherwise, don't bother reading the rest—just try to color between the lines and turn your children over to the proper authorities immediately.

Socialization

Can't We All Just Get Along?

BY "SOCIALIZATION," I'M NOT TALKING ABOUT THE EXCELLENT medical system in Canada but rather about behavior that works in our society. Get an early start on this one, because personality is a tough area in which to play catch-up. (Once a jerk, always a jerk.) Years from now, you don't want to be living with a miserable teen, disliked by his mates, because you'll be more than inconvenienced; you'll be heartbroken at his rejection.

POPULAR OPINION

TO BE HAPPY, YOUR KID WILL NEED TO BE ACCEPTED AND, BEYOND that, popular. Kids find their own popularity points in areas like sports, money, fashion, and sex. I know you didn't want to hear that last one, and you're probably as disturbed as the rest of us that "bookworm" never seems to make the list. If you figure out how to raise a popular nerd, write a book yourself. In the meantime, try to keep academic pursuits on your child's radar and convince him there will be time for other indulgences.

TO HAVE A FRIEND, BE A FRIEND

THAT OLD SAYING IS ONE OF THE NUGGETS WE PARENTS HAND down. Hopefully, you have a few friends yourself so you'll have some credibility here.

There are tactics you can teach: point out that people like to hear phrases like, "As you said…" and "I agree that…" and others that make it sound like you're being agreeable even as you're about to go off on your own tangent. I had a friend who used to say, "That's a silly argument" and "You're wrong." I'm not sure if he said that to everybody or just to me, but it was off-putting; these are not the kinds of buzzwords that warm people up to you. In the adult world, asking people about themselves and giving them space to talk makes you seem like a really interesting guy by the end of dinner, and it doesn't hurt on the playground either.

TIPS

A) DON'T CHOOSE HIS FRIENDS. SOME OF HIS CHOICES WILL be horrific, but they're his own: the bully, the wuss, the tattletale, the smart-ass, the brat. On second thought…

b) Choose his friends! Do whatever is necessary to weed out the bad seeds, and plan playdates with children whose behavior you'd have him emulate. And racial diversity is an important concept in the global community of his or her future.

c) Don't be judgmental. Your child's standards of behavior with his peers will be one generation removed from yours: new slang, new fashion, new interests. Within reason, let him make his own choices.

d) Be judgmental! Now and 'til the day you die. That's your prerogative and your responsibility, and you have years of experience on him. If he truly knows as much as you do, either you've screwed up or he's a genius.

e) Be his friend. Be someone he can talk to about anything. Here's where it gets complicated, because the next piece of advice is...

f) Don't be his friend! Find your own best friend. Dads can become best friends later, but early on there's a lot of teaching to be done, and your child needs an omniscient figure whose decisions he can count on. His equals don't give him that. You're another dimension, a superior being. Don't lower yourself to a more plebeian status.

g) Don't burst his bubbles. He's a kid. He'll grow up soon enough and hear the cold truth about the Easter Bunny and the Tooth Fairy, and at some point one of his heroes will let him down—guntoting basketball players and horny presidents come to mind—and he'll see the fine line between fact and fantasy. We did a *Growing Pains* episode in which Dad took Ben backstage to meet a rock idol, only to witness some awful behavior—spousal and substance abuse. The dilemma was whether to expose the bum or let his son hold on to his icons. What would you do?

h) Burst those bubbles! Bust 'em up good. Let him see people for who they really are, warts and all, and get him ready for the riff-raff element. Just be sure to let him know that when the rest have turned their backs, you will always be there for him—always.

i) Push him to succeed. You'll give him confidence.

j) Don't push the kid! You'll make him neurotic. Aw hell, push him! If he survives your parenting, he can handle anything. Most of the time, father knows best, and there are occasions when a kid does need to be pushed. That hippie-dippie, airy-fairy, artsy-fartsy, wishy-washy parenting style of a generation ago can be too loosey-goosey, laissez faire, hands-on/hands-off in cases where you know your kid should try something that doesn't appeal to him at first, peas and liver excepted. Your child may not like the sound of signing up for soccer, karate, choir, Boy Scouts, or Sunday school, but there's a good chance he'll love it if you can trick him into showing up.

COOLISH OR FOOLISH?

SHOULD A PARENT TRY TO BE POPULAR WITH SCHOOLMATES? Robin and Brennan had very different feelings about introducing me to their chums. Robin milked it as a door opener because Dad was on a popular TV show, whereas Brennan wanted to carve his own independent path. Carter is jealous of people asking for autographs but enjoys the perks, like free stuff at movie premieres.

Your first-grader will tell you when you're helping and when you're simply being a geeky embarrassment, so pay attention, take his cue, and be responsive to his peculiar sensibilities.

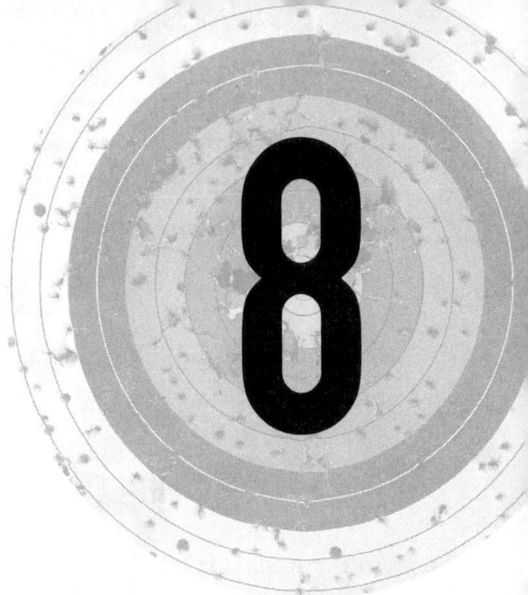

Discipline

When Good Kids Go Bad

THE WINDBAG SYNDROME

ACCORDING TO PEDIATRICIAN BURTON WHITE, THERE'S NO point in disciplining kids under seven months old. First, your child isn't capable of understanding that he's doing something wrong. Second, babies under seven months have short memories, and by the time your baby has been reprimanded, he'll have already forgotten what he did to get you upset.

When your lecture drones into its second hour, you've long since been tuned out. Save your breath—shorter is better.

JUST SAY "NO!"

THE FIRST TIME YOU ATTEMPT TO TEACH THE CONCEPT OF "no," it will probably have something to do with the fact that kids like to touch dangerous things—or, worse, expensive things.

You've always had a plan for how you would discipline your child—how firmness and fairness would guide you to be the perfect cop—but did you plan for his first wordless tantrum? He's at an advantage here, because he's the only one who speaks his language. You're going to have your hands full trying to interpret, control, and then satisfy his emotions.

THREE LITTLE RULES

THESE SHOULD ESTABLISH THE LAWS OF THE LAND AT AN EARLY AGE.

1. Obey quickly.
2. Talk nicely.
3. Show the love.

Later on, you can try to explain the "why." For now, "Just do as you're told!" will do.

OBSTREPEROUS

THAT'S A GOOD DESCRIPTION OF THE EVIL TWIN WHO occasionally takes over your angel's persona around age five. They've always had the temperament; they just didn't have the words. Now they do. Prepare to do battle, draw your sword, man the drawbridge, and damn the torpedoes. While it's true it takes a village to raise a child, a village with an army would be even better.

THE "WHY" FACTOR

YOU CAN EXPLAIN TO YOUR TODDLER THAT YOU'RE MAKING A decision based on their safety and health. That will make sense, but don't assume your kids will always listen just because you're older, bigger, and louder. After age five they will need more expansive reasons, and you will find yourself challenged to offer more esoteric explanations for your rules and regulations. Some might even be religious or spiritual, including the fear of God. ("You can't play with that urn because your grandmother's in there.")

Sadly, your kid's respect for you is no longer automatic. You'll have to earn it by proving over and over again that you make as much sense as all of the other influences in the world combined, hereinafter known as Worldly Influences.

I made the mistake of taking Carter on a frightening roller coaster when he was four and telling him it would be fun. It was not—he hated every terrifying second—and afterwards it took a while to win back his trust. When I would make a decision on something he was originally skittish toward, but about which I proved to be right (such as going to Sea World and feeding the beluga whale), I would brag to him, "That was a good call." After a few good calls, he knew he could count on me, and I could be the taller, stronger genius once again.

NEGOTIATION

HOUSEHOLD RULES ARE NON-NEGOTIABLE, BUT IF A DISAGREEment is a matter of opinion, let him win once in a while, for crying out loud! It's no skin off your nose, and you already win by default because in addition to older/bigger/louder, you have the car keys. My money's on you, Bucko.

Most importantly, you're also smarter than he is (honest!), so find a way for both of you to win the debate. Outflank him and STOP THE MADNESS now by using the strategy "Don't Go to Bed Mad: Kid Version."

To defuse the tension, you might follow a simple three-step Defensive Parenting plan:

1. *Kid the kid.* When trouble seems imminent, start softly by using the "humor and cajole" technique. Use words and facial expressions to imply, "That's funny, son. I know you can't be serious," and give him a moment to rethink his position and bail out of his argument.

2. *Mano a mano.* If he persists, go eye-to-eye with him and make him restate his beef, this time understanding that there may be punishment if eye-to-eye becomes toe-to-toe and he loses—which he must! You're no longer laughing, but if you change the subject, you can come back to the problematic one when he's distracted from his anger. I've always liked this method, because it allows everyone a little face-saving wiggle room, and if it's not exactly win-win, at least it's not lose-lose.

3. *Lower the boom.* If "cajole" and "distract" have failed, you are at Level Orange on the Homeland Threat color chart. You have walked that fine line between nurturing and enabling and given it your rational best; now your child must learn that there are limits to your patience. If you save your booming Zeus voice and Rasputin face for this Last Straw Big Finish, you should be able to avoid the Mega Meltdown—both his and, more stressfully, yours.

THE JOSE APPROACH

AS IN "NO WAY, JOSE." A MORE GROWN-UP VERSION OF "JUST DO as you're told!" this is an expression of firmness that worked in our generation even for kids not named Jose. It was unequivocal…undeniable…non-negotiable…fuggedaboudit…"What is it you don't understand about the word 'no'?"…all rolled into one.

HOLD YOUR NO'S

AS CHILDREN GET OLDER, SAVE YOUR ABSOLUTE NO'S FOR the important things. If you don't like your children's clothes or hairdo, express your opinion modestly and then agree to disagree and look the other way, if necessary—but only out of one eye. Then they'll know that "no means no" when they hear it.

TRUTH OR CONSEQUENCES

KIDS NEED TO KNOW THAT THERE ARE CONSEQUENCES FOR THEIR behavior. Try to avoid making the consequences sound like threats all the time, but your child should know when a special trip to the park is at stake. You lose your toys, your bike, your television privileges, and your telephone time if you don't finish your homework. If you really need to push the envelope, consider playing the classic material deprivation (aka the "Santa Claus Is Coming To Town") card: no presents.

You'd better have serious consequences in mind when school comes into your life. In the first week of the first grade, Carter came home and expressed his opinion that it would be no big deal if he was made to go to the principal's office because he wasn't paying attention in class. He quickly learned that it would be a very big deal and that he would probably spend the rest of his natural life alone and naked with a bowl of rice and a glass of water in the corner of a dark room with no Gameboy or MP3 player.

WHEN TO DISCIPLINE

SHOULD YOU DISCIPLINE THE KID IMMEDIATELY, RIGHT THERE on the spot, or later on? We were in the parking lot at the Hollywood Park racetrack—not Carter's usual weekend hangout, but we were there for a Kids' Fundraiser. The paparazzi were there, so when Carter became cranky, I tried to be charming and laugh off the fact that he wouldn't smile for the photographer or play nice. He was a little turd, actually. Then he upped the ante by hitting, whining, and pulling away—playfully, I like to think (OK, I'm in denial)—and headed back to the car. I didn't feel it was necessary to make a scene at that moment because, unlike the two-year-olds who won't remember what they did wrong ten minutes ago, these five-year-olds are in the Big Leagues, and they'll know what's coming when it arrives an hour later. It's the old "Wait 'til your father gets home" tactic: a little anticipation and fear never hurt anyone.

Use your parental instincts about the magnitude of the crime when deciding how immediate and dramatic your response should be.

P.S. When we got home, I packed up some of his toys as a donation to the children's fund. He remembers that to this day, and we have never had another bad scene at the racetrack.

WHEN IS IT OK TO BITE YOUR COUSIN?

WHEN:

a) She bites first.
b) No one's watching.
c) You're really, really hungry.

Well, it's never right, which is why you want to teach your kids to walk away before a dispute escalates to war. In a biting scenario, immediate fallout is required, or else an hour later the aunt and uncle will be all over you.

THE PINOCCHIO EFFECT

NO AMOUNT OF RELIGIOUS UPBRINGING, DISCIPLINE, OR ROLE modeling will get you through an entire adolescence without your child lying to you. It might be a little white one or a big whopper, but rest assured, you will be deceived on some matter large or small.

Expect to get the runaround when you ask:

- Did you take a piece of gum?
- Did you hit Spencer?
- Have you finished your homework?
- Were you touching yourself when I walked in?
- Was anyone drinking at the party?
- Are you sexually active?

Breaking the ice on subjects like these is difficult for both the iceberg and the icebreaker. You're trying to get information, but you're smart enough to know that you can't be overly judgmental, accusatory, inflammatory, or punitive right out of the gate; otherwise, you will forever discourage honest dialogue about these subjects. By the same token, the very asking of the question reminds your boy or girl that there are boundaries, and that there are repercussions for those who violate them. Questions like, "Have you ever smoked weed?" are best disguised in the midst of a conversation in which they think you're a friend. When you've got them sucked in and comfortable, remind them you're a parent and hit them with the Inquisition. There are no instances in recorded history of a child stepping forward and volunteering such information. "Oh, hi, Dad. Come on in. I was just watching porn on the Internet." "Hey, Mom, sorry you were asleep when I got home last night. You should have seen Jason at the party—whacked out of his gourd on Jägermeister and barfing all over Mrs. Falwell's new sofa."

Never forget: it's your house, and your prerogative to introduce these topics and keep up-to-date on them.

THE GOLDEN JET

WHAT FOLLOWS IS A LONG, WHIMSICAL ANECDOTE THAT YOU should read only if you have the time.

In my career as a duplicitous, deceitful, sneaky, lying fraud, I was a late bloomer. It wasn't until my second year at university that I pulled off a classic that lasted the entire school year. Technically speaking, it was not a lie, but rather an omission. My first year of college at the University of Western Ontario in London had been way too much fun, and my B-minus average was not what my parents had had in mind. Consequently, in my second year, I was forbidden to have a car. In my freshman year I had lived in a student residence, so I hadn't needed one. I was also in a divinity/theology curriculum, so I really didn't need one. (There was no place I could go where some saint wouldn't be watching.) However, things changed in my second year, and I wanted a car. In defiance of my parents' order, I secretly bought a 1957 gold-painted Volkswagen Beetle for $300. (Digression within a digression: Remind me to tell you about a prized souvenir I still possess: the $5.00 ticket stub to see the Beatles at Maple Leaf Gardens in 1966. Come to think of it, maybe you'll see it on eBay someday if the S&P 500 tanks again.) My vehicle was affectionately known among my friends as the Golden Jet, a moniker borrowed from '60s Hall of Fame hockey legend Bobby Hull. I happily tooled around campus and the city of London, Ontario, in this fuel-efficient beauty and was fortunate to not have any unannounced visits from my parents during the school year. On those occasions when I knew they were coming, the Golden Jet simply stayed in the hangar and I would hitchhike. (If you can remember the days when hitchhiking was safe and commonplace, you may also have a $5.00 Beatles ticket stub.) But the Golden Jet gained legendary status with one particular excursion in the stone-cold Canadian winter month of February.

PROM STRATEGY

IF YOU HAD A STEADY GIRLFRIEND, YOU WERE OBLIGED TO escort her to the Snow Ball. Otherwise, it was best to use this special occasion to take someone you'd longed for but hadn't dated yet, because an invitation to the prom says, "I mean business, baby!" My buddy John and I had big plans that year, including a reservation at the Peter Pan Motel, anticipating that we'd show our dates such a great time that they'd want to join us there for an after-party. We had the requisite lemon gin and 7-Up and were looking good in our rented tuxedos. The only flaw in the plan was how badly we overestimated our dates' interest in us. To make a long story short (or is it too late?), by 2 a.m., the girls were hardly under our spell and insisted on a ride home. Immediately! These were the kind of girls you hope your daughter will be. By 2:15 a.m. we found ourselves sitting alone in our tuxes, mildly intoxicated, and freezing our asses off in 20-below temperatures—outside and inside, as the Golden Jet was not famous for its heater. There were always a few geeks back at the dorm who took pleasure in waiting to see which losers returned earliest from parties like these, and we had no intention of being those losers.

FLORIDARIN

WHAT FOLLOWED WAS ONE OF THE MOST CREATIVE AND far-flung adventures of our young careers as losers. John and I and the Golden Jet set out for Fort Lauderdale, in the far-off, unreachable, unimaginably mysterious American state of Florida! This was right up there with Lewis and Clark, given that we had less than $100, neither of us knew exactly where Florida was, and we smelled like lemon gin. On the road out of town by 3 a.m., we arrived twenty-seven hours later in the land of fifteen-cent burgers and began an adventure that would last a week, bunking at a dorm at the University of Miami and enjoying the hospitality of a couple of coeds who were willing to pass the time in ways those prom dates back home refused to. We even met two crazy schoolteachers from New Jersey who offered to teach us a variety of things apparently considered normal in New Jersey—and only in New Jersey.

While John partied, I, being the more mature and sophisticated of the two, decided to explore the local culture one night by signing up for a blue-haired ladies bus tour of the Deavulle Hotel Revue. It was like Vegas in those days, with all the top performers appearing in big showrooms, and for $14.95 you could get two watered-down drinks and see Bobby Darin from a standing-room-only position at the back. I did just that and saw my idol perform, and seven years later I was beyond thrilled to be hired as a writer on Bobby's NBC series.

It was a great week in Florida, and upon returning I felt enough guilt over the Golden Jet that I almost decided to tell my parents. I chickened out at the last minute, and to this day I've never had this conversation with my father. (This is me 'fessing up, Dad.) I was a good enough kid, however, to realize that I had been dishonest and dodged a bullet. I remained uncomfortable about that secret, and that discomfort probably prevented me from doing anything that sneaky again.

In summary, your kids will lie to you and you may never find out. The amoral liar thinks, "Hey, that worked. I'll keep trying it," and becomes an inveterate fibber and criminal-in-training. If you've raised your kids smartly and kept "right from wrong" on their radar, however, they will share your value system, feel badly about their mistakes, and be less inclined to repeat their transgressions.

RETURN THE BOOK NOW AND GET A REFUND

THERE ARE NO BOOKS—NOT EVEN THIS ONE—THAT CAN guarantee perfect results in raising children. It's an inexact science with one gigantic variable: children! Many of our problems will be imaginary or at least exaggerated, exacerbated by our well-intentioned paranoia as parents. Some unexpected behavior, however, will be real and will require special attention.

THE SCHOOL BULLY

YOU WILL BE BETTER OFF IF YOUR SON IS THE BULLY-EE AND NOT the bully-er, the victim and not the aggressor. The aggressor's parents may have their hands full with larger issues, ones that Band-Aids won't fix.

I've heard people-in-the-know like Ann Pleshette Murphy (*Good Morning America*, *Family Circle*) tell us we shouldn't add to a son's burden by turning against him. He wants to feel that you are working as his advocate at school to find out what's going on. This is an early lesson in the concept of "innocent until proven guilty."

Some children become bullies because they have been teased themselves or because they are having trouble expressing difficult emotions. If he opens up and complains about other kids, be sure to listen. Make him see that you're on his side, but let him know that picking on others is never acceptable.

And another thing: watch your own behavior at home. When parents discipline harshly or inconsistently, if they relentlessly criticize or belittle, they create a bully-making environment. Boost his self-esteem through after-school activities or by assigning tasks around the house that he can be successful at in a grown-up, responsible way.

THE TEENAGE CRIMINAL

A CRIME IS A CRIME IS A CRIME. DON'T TEACH YOUR CHILD THAT he can decide what should be legal and what laws deserve to be broken. The drinking age, marijuana laws, and driving restrictions are more than "suggestions" and "guidelines."

PETTY THEFT

ON THE STEALING FRONT, WHEN I WAS TWELVE, I WAS AT A small convenience store and a pack of gum was calling out my name. The owner promised not to tell my parents if I promised never to come into that store again. Done deal. End of story.

GET THE KID A SHRINK THE MINUTE HE CAN SIT UP

NO ONE QUESTIONS THE VALUE OF TRAINED COUNSELORS, psychiatrists, and psychologists. What is open to debate is the nature and extent of therapy: short-term specific or long-term generic? Brennan and his mom insisted that weekly counseling was important to deal with some broken-home issues, so he attended during school months, which allowed him to skip class once a week for sessions. When the summer holiday arrived, however, all anxieties seemed to magically disappear and nary another appointment was needed. Was school itself the culprit?

Another debate concerns the possibility of over-diagnosis. In this case, dependency on therapy becomes a self-fulfilling prophecy.

Shop for a counselor as you would for a new car: kick the tires and learn about that counselor's approach to make sure that you agree.

Kids are being diagnosed with bipolar disorder, ADHD, obsessive-compulsive disorder, social-anxiety disorder, post-traumatic stress disorder, pathological impulsiveness, sleeplessness, phobias, and more. In the good old days, it was bed-wetting and talking with your mouth full.

WHEN DR. PHIL ISN'T ENOUGH

FOR SERIOUS CONCERNS, THE AMERICAN ACADEMY OF CHILD and Adolescent Psychiatry lists dozens of psychotropic medications available for troubled kids, from Ritalin (for ADHD) to Zoloft (for depression), as well as stimulants, mood stabilizers, sleep medications, anticonvulsants, antipsychotics, and anti-anxieties, which you might not know from anti-aircraft, antipasta, or Auntie Mame, so ask questions. The increasing incidence of psychopathology in young people is probably the result of better diagnosis and detection working hand in hand with that old bugaboo, parental paranoia.

FACTOID

10 percent of all American kids may suffer from some mental illness, and twice that many have exhibited some signs of depression.

GENERATION RX: GIVE THOUGHT A CHANCE

ARE WE MEDDLING WITH NORMAL PROGRESSION? WHAT DO PSYCHOtropic drugs do to still-developing brains that have years to go before being fully formed?

Consensus seems to be that Lexapro is the perfect answer for anxiety—provided you're willing to overlook the fact that it artificially manipulates the chemicals responsible for feeling and thought. Likewise,

Adderall is the perfect answer for ADHD—provided you ignore the fact that it's a stimulant like Dexedrine and has left youngsters with side effects such as weight loss and sleeplessness.

For children with less severe symptoms—children who are somber but not depressed, antsy but not clinically hyperactive, who rely on some repetitive behaviors for comfort but are not patently obsessive-compulsive—the pros and cons of using drugs are less obvious. Stephen Hinshaw, chairman of psychology at the University of California–Berkeley, worries that we might start medicating normal variations in behavior, noting that, "The world would be a far less interesting place if all the eccentric kids were medicated toward some golden mean."

What does psychopharmacological meddling do to the acquisition of emotional skills when anti-anxiety drugs are prescribed for a child who has not yet acquired life experience and the means of managing stress without the meds? We know from imaging studies that the frontal lobes, which are vital to management functions like channeling feelings and thought, don't fully mature until age thirty—and much later in network executives and wide receivers.

FACTOID

Some new meds have been developed specifically for kids, but most have been approved for adults only and are not recommended for use at children's doses: kids are not merely little adults; they metabolize medications differently.

SNOOZE OR LOSE?

DO YOU WATCH A PROBLEM DEVELOP OR INTERVENE AND AIM to prevent the disorder? Treating kids who are not yet truly sick is controversial because there's a chance they might not develop the condition at all. In the future, we hope to know more about genetics and biological markers to better predict the direction kids are headed in, and MRIs may determine if medications are doing damage.

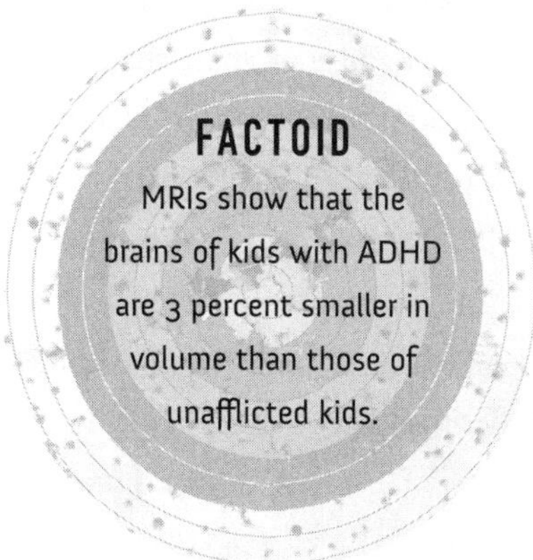

FACTOID
MRIs show that the brains of kids with ADHD are 3 percent smaller in volume than those of unafflicted kids.

BUT WHAT IF WE DO NOTHING?

THOSE WITH UNTREATED DEPRESSION HAVE A LIFETIME suicide rate of 15 percent. Kids with severe and untreated ADHD have been linked to a higher rate of substance abuse, a higher dropout rate, and more trouble with the law. Some bipolar kids have a tendency to injure or kill themselves, while others engage in destructive behaviors like brawling and reckless driving.

In puberty, bouts of depression are typical, but if they last two weeks or more the child may need treatment. A new school or neighborhood may be a welcome change to some children, but they may aggravate an existing sense of vulnerability in others. Help kids learn to put things in perspective.

If you don't, one anxiety may trigger another, and they can only handle so many crises before they crack. Above all, take suicide threats seriously. Approximately 300 youths between ten and fourteen will commit suicide in America this year.

H.M.O. B.S.

ONE OF THE CONSENSUS CULPRITS IN THE HURRY-UP-AND-DRUG-THEM culture is managed care, which is already disinclined to pay for talk therapy because it takes longer and costs more than pills. In a perfect world, parents considering meds for their kids would have access to not only one specialist but three: a pediatrician, a behavioral pediatrician, and a child-adolescent psychiatrist.

There will always be hazards associated with taking too many drugs—and, in some cases, dangers from taking too few. The most powerful medicine a suffering child can get is the educated instinct of a well-informed parent.

Role Models

Mr. and Mrs. Perfect

"No one is totally worthless; you can always be used as a bad example."

– Proverb for flunkies

ARE YOU PREPARED TO BE A POP IDOL, AS IN "POP, YOU'RE MY IDOL"?

IT'S EASY TO LIST THE AREAS IN WHICH YOU AFFECT YOUR CHILD, but what of his impact on you? Powerful! Your newborn is now your main validation in life.

Who he becomes will be a measure of what you were.

You want to get this job done right, and that means accepting that his most important role model is you.

His concept of what a man and woman are will be what the two of you show him.

Your political opinions, social behavior, work ethic, and parenting skills are being studied. Are you prepared to have your baby know you that well?

WHO ARE YOU, ANYWAY?

WHAT WILL HE LEARN FROM YOU ABOUT LANGUAGE, GRAMMAR, hospitality, manners, morality, and family?

What will he see in you that will help him understand fear, pain, self-control, and faith?

If you want him to share your feelings about academics and careers, what examples will you set? And what will you teach him about love and, yes (gulp!), sexuality?

Don't impose your own eccentricities on him, but rather expose him to everything you like—the hobbies, music, and sports you've enjoyed—while still encouraging him to develop his own identity by engaging in his own unique blend of interests. Let him know that he will be more appealing to others if he has a few colorful oddities in his repertoire, if he strays off the beaten path, not always doing what the other kids are doing, not always following the crowd—or you. His specialties will become conversation starters. I didn't drink at all in high school, for instance, and that was very unusual in my town. I made up for it all in one regrettable night in college, however. (Remind me to tell you the "head-out-the-car-window-like-a-dog" story when I see you in person.) I have been a quasi-teetotaler ever since.

For my musical identity, I didn't play the oboe or guitar but…bagpipes! Your kids don't have to go that far to be different.

The environment your child lives in will also set standards for his early taste in material things, including his appreciation of art, homes, furnishings, décor, and cars. You'll influence his look, the way he dresses and grooms himself. Have you learned anything from the *Queer Eye* bunch? Not that you can expect him to dress like you—that would be peer suicide—but by observing you he will notice that there are dress codes in life, acceptable and unacceptable ways to dress for school (thank God for uniform rules that eliminate his choices), birthday parties, restaurants, Sunday dinner at Grandma's, and everything else. The current definition of "formal" seems to mean a collared shirt. Where I grew up—in the remote permafrost township of Kirkland Lake—"formal" meant your fly was done up.

You might want to rethink your entire wardrobe, put away your clown clothes, and set some style examples. But don't go too far—nothing is more dorky than a middle-aged man trying to dress like a teenager. What is a dork? You'll know it when you're being one—your kid might even tell you when it's happening.

DAVY CROCKETT WAS A SONOFABITCH

THE FIRST FAD I FOLLOWED WAS THE DISNEY-DRIVEN DAVY Crockett phenomenon, during which I had to have the coonskin cap and jacket, unaware of how politically incorrect that would be today on several levels: wearing an animal, killing Injuns, taking land from the Mexicans. Davy Crockett was a bastard!

SUDDENLY TEENAGE

YOUR KIDS ARE TRYING THE SAME STUNTS YOU DID, ONLY they're smarter. Or not. When my boys were teenagers, I returned from a weekend out of town to discover empty vodka bottles in the garbage cans outside. Fortunately, they acknowledged a "little party" before I busted them. The culprits, of course, were some kids they didn't know who showed up uninvited, were asked to leave, and apparently dumped their empty bottles outside. Nice try.

WE'RE NOT WORTHY!

WE'VE ALL HEARD SOME PARENT SAY, "IF MY KID WANTS TO DRINK or smoke, he can do it at home in front of me." Some parents who catch their kid smoking or drinking confront those troublesome temptations by forcing the child to sit down and polish off a pack or a quart—a tactic that may well work, although I've never met anyone who's actually done it.

What is your take on tobacco, alcohol, and drugs? Is it, "Just say no," or is partying at home with friends OK? Will you forbid pot smoking once your son or daughter is living on their own at college? Are you being a hypocrite in any of the above areas? How will you answer if they know you've done it and they ask you if it was fun?

I will never forget one Monday morning in mid-winter, when a classmate in the twelfth grade failed to show up for school. He had not been seen since leaving a party Friday night. There was much tension in the classroom as we were interrogated, first by teachers, then by police. Larry didn't show up the next day either, nor was he seen again for the remainder of the school year. Months later, one spring afternoon, I came home from school to find my father waiting at the kitchen table, looking as glum as I had ever seen him. As the doctor in the community, he had been on call earlier that day when a lady reported spotting an arm protruding from the melting snow while she was hanging out the laundry on her back porch. Larry had apparently had too much to drink and tried to take a shortcut home through some backyards. He probably got lost and passed out or fell asleep. The world is scarier now that we've added drugs and weapons to our youth culture.

"NO POT UNTIL THE FIRST GRADE"

TO THE LIST OF EMBARRASSING DAD GOOFS, LET ME ADD THIS one. It was the early '80s, and we were all still hung over from those crazy '70s. I was married to Gloria Loring, that talented and beautiful soap star, recording artist, and mother of my two eldest sons. We had a small party at our house one Saturday night, and one generous guest, deciding to go beyond the traditional bottle of wine, left a little something extra in the refrigerator: remarkable homemade baked goods, along with a note saying "from the Robinsons"—not their real names, since I'm not sure if the statute of limitations applies here. Fast-forward to Monday morning, when I received a call from my sons' school reporting that something was amiss and that I should pick them up.

When I arrived, the boys seemed strangely happy, though unusually tired. Neither of them, ages four and six, had their perky preschool and kindergarten game faces on; in fact, they barely seemed to recognize me. Maybe that's why they were smiling. I learned that each of them, in separate classrooms, had fallen asleep, their heads on their desks, at almost precisely the same time. After a curious ride home I led them to their respective beds, where they were bent on taking a nap. Immediately. My instincts led me to the refrigerator, and upon further investigation I confirmed my wildest speculation. My preschoolers had raided the fridge and eaten the pot brownies on their way to school! As far as I know, there was never a recurrence of this incident, as weed treats never did catch on as the snack of choice in our household. The Robinsons are, I believe, now growing hemp somewhere in Oregon.

NOT IN FRONT OF THE KIDS!

YOUR CHILD DOES NOT NEED TO SEE A SPOUSAL DEBATE escalate into a national incident. Agree on a signal with your mate for when the conversation is going too far, something like "raincheck," to indicate you'll continue the discussion later.

Plan to abandon these ruses before your child reaches age five, and don't even think that spelling out obscenities will work. He can spell when he wants to, and it will be earlier than you think.

THE INFALLIBLE YOU

WHEN YOU BEHAVE BADLY YOURSELF, DON'T WAIT FOR YOUR child to bust you at a time that suits him. It may be ten years down the road before he makes his harsh assessment in the context of everything he's learned in the interim. His epiphany may not even come until he's a father himself, at which time he will look at your behavior all those years ago and come to the conclusion that you were, at that moment, a donkey. Feel free to nip his admonishment in the bud by admitting your mistake and providing an appropriate explanation. Parents don't need to be perfect. In fact, teaching kids a lesson in humility by owning up to your own shortcomings is a worthwhile exercise. If you can take it a step further and even find some bemusement in your confession, you'll be applauded for exhibiting a self-deprecating sense of humor. (I once did a show that was unanimously despised by critics—except for one, whose review was less vile. Unfortunately, while trying to pay me a compliment, my only fan proved to be a functional illiterate. He wrote, "Alan Thicke has a nice, self-defecating sense of humor.")

THE MOST HEROIC THING MY DAD EVER DID

OF ALL THE IMAGES WE'D LOVE TO BE KNOWN FOR, SURELY being a hero in our child's eyes tops the list. Not all of us can be firemen or soldiers, much less ninja warriors or NFL quarterbacks, but my dad once put on an old-fashioned swashbuckling display of courage that resonates in my memory today. As a nine-year-old, I ran home crying one afternoon because some big kids had taken my football and wouldn't give it back. They were tossing it around, teasing me in a manner deserving of a fifteen-yard taunting penalty. Dad stormed to the park, even more furious than I was, and ran after these punks as they continued to play keep-away, until they finally left the ball in the middle of the field and ran off, either intimidated by my father's rancor or afraid they'd be charged with murder when he died of a heart attack. Flushed and breathless, he handed the ball back to me, looking for all the world like Superman and Brett Favre rolled into one. Thanks, Dad.

MENTORS

THERE ARE TIMES WHEN THE BEST ADVICE A KID CAN GET is to give up.

I was fortunate to have been mentored by caring adults whose wisdom and analysis led me from one key juncture to another on my life's path. Mostly, I've had a career by default, in which somebody was always kind enough to tell me that I sucked at something and should switch direction. At six, my piano teacher told my mother to save her money and get me a paper route, where the skill level of my hands could be put to better use.

In the ninth grade, my high school football coach advised that I was too small, too slow, and too timid to make the squad, and that perhaps I should consider another activity, like playing the piano. In my senior year, I tried infiltrating a local rock band and was told I might be good at something other than singing, like loading amplifiers onto a truck.

As a teenager, when I thought I was ready to lose my virginity—no, I knew I was ready to lose my virginity—my first fumbling attempt was greeted with mild laughter and the suggestion that, once again, my hands would be better suited to another hobby, although Denise didn't stick around long enough to make a specific recommendation.

After a very active childhood in the United Church of Canada, I was contemplating entering the ministry, until my preacher suggested that God and I weren't ready for each other on a full-time basis.

As a young adult who had achieved some success in regional hockey, I was advised by no less an expert than Bobby Orr—yes, the one in Chapter 3—to abandon my aspirations to try out for the World Hockey Association and stick with my recreational league because I was too small, too slow, and too timid. He could have been a football coach.

In my thirties, fresh from the success of an afternoon talk show, I tried a late-night program called *Thicke of the Night* and was informed by the entire population of the United States that I was not cut out for a challenge to Johnny Carson. Respected critic Tom Shales mentioned in a humiliating national column that I seemed to be a nice fellow and should try a vocation more suited to my skills—like farming.

In show business, I've been rejected for jobs I didn't even want. Talk about embarrassment! Honest advice can be a cold business, but one exceptional mentor stands out among all the discouragers. His name was Ernie Dixon, and he was my high school principal. Mr. Dixon would have preferred to develop a star quarterback for the Elliot Lake High School team, but our town was small, and the team reeked, so his only hope of any recognition for his students was in the domain of oratory—public speaking, as we called it—where he hoped to nurture an orator skilled enough to compete in regional contests. I became the putty Mr. Dixon hoped to mold, and he began patiently coaching me in an empty classroom every day at 4 p.m., honing my writing and speaking styles until I was ready for competition. He would then personally drive me hundreds of miles to that weekend's speech contest. I even managed to win a few, which pleased him. I will always be grateful for his confidence and sacrifice, and we have stayed in touch ever since. Mr. Dixon even interrupted his retirement to motor down from northern Ontario to southern California to attend one of my weddings. Thank you, sir. You are not forgotten.

"When I was a boy of fourteen, my father was so ignorant I could hardly stand to have the old man around. But when I got to be twenty-one, I was astonished at how much he had learned in seven years."

– Mark Twain

SHOW BUSINESS

(One of the fringe benefits is that you get to introduce your relatives to famous people!)

Mom, Flip, and Will

Rock Hudson with (my) sister Joanne and brother Todd

Ali, Robin, me, and the Governator

Yes, that's Elvis with Todd!

A president not sharing ice cream

Ole Blue Eyes

Backstage: Nephew Creighton, Beyoncé, Niece Victoria and friend, Total Stranger

Jeremy Piven, Tanya, Will Ferrell at The Goods *Premiere*

Peer Pressure

Slackers, Divas, Thugs, Trollops, and Thieves

THERE IS A WHOLE WORLD OF ROLE MODELING GOING ON OUTSIDE the comfortable confines of your house. Bad adults are one thing, but when your children start looking up to other kids, be very afraid. What if the kid being emulated has worse parents than you?

From Ron Taffel's *The Second Family: How Adolescent Power Is Challenging the American Family* (St. Martin's Press): "Peer pressure is at its most intense between fifth and eighth grade but can begin as early as first and second."

Eleanor Roosevelt on self-esteem: "No one can make you feel inferior without your consent."

We touched on how your tastes influence your child's early sense of fashion, and that's worth holding onto for as long as possible, in spite of the potential damage to your credit rating. Females are especially susceptible to the marketing appeal of a brand name—guys are more attracted to beer labels—and although I know of no studies that pinpoint when this phenomenon kicks in, mothers could probably identify the year, day, store, and outfit that first hooked them.

LABEL ENVY (AKA PRADA COVETUS)

THIS, AFTER ALL, IS A GENDER-SPECIFIC TRAIT, AS YOU'LL SEE on any shopping trip when a woman must have a designer handbag or shoes—because Reese Witherspoon has the exact same kind. One of my wives was a centipede and it would have been cheaper to wrap her feet in $100 bills. Men aren't like this. We don't show up at a party and gush, "Where did you get those loafers? And where can I find a wallet like that?" Everything I own has a corporate logo on it. Guys get free swag at golf tournaments—free sports bags, free sneakers, and free key chains. Go with it. Enjoy it, and teach your boys that it's important that guys get things for free so they have money left over for women and their handbags. It's bad enough when women teach this behavior to their daughters, but when they try to teach it to their sons, all hell can break loose. Some mothers would dress their son in a button-down shirt when a pullover would be more than adequate at the birthday party he's going to, where he will play dodgeball and pick up caterpillars and spill Kool Aid—the red kind. Practicality is Dad's lesson; fashion is Mom's.

Okay, okay. The truth is, girls are simply better when it comes to looking nice. They raise the bar, and we love them for it.

Fashion is an important way for kids to express themselves and one they should be allowed to pursue within reason. Even boys develop an acute brand consciousness by age ten, and more than 80 percent have a favorite brand of sneaker. (Nike by a mile!) In summary: While you might require that stiff shirt and those shiny shoes for Sunday-night dinners at grandma's, don't make your child into your mini-me. You have your own wardrobe.

THE THING ABOUT THONGS

AS IF WE NEEDED ONE EXTRA POINT OF CONTENTION BETWEEN us and our preteen and teenage daughters, another has come along in recent years: underwear. Don't even suggest underpants from Jockey or Hanes—which your daughters call Granny Panties—when every girl at school is wearing a thong.

How can they be so important, you may well ask, when no one is supposed to see them? There's a real short list of people who should see your underwear on any given day, and you'll want to know who's on that list. Hopefully, no surprises. A vice principal at a San Diego high school was demoted after she lifted the girls' skirts for an undies inspection before allowing them into a school dance. That practice hasn't caught on.

ANOTHER THING ABOUT THONGS

SALES OF THONGS TO TWEENS (THE AGE SEVEN TO TWELVE bracket) have quadrupled since 2000. Girls ages thirteen to seventeen spend a shocking percentage of their overall clothing budget on underpants. I read 40 percent in one report. Mom, could that possibly be true? Not when there are girls in underprivileged countries who have no thongs at all! Does underpant obsession signal moral bankruptcy? Developmental psychologist Deborah Tolman says in *Dilemmas of Desire: Teenage Girls Talk about Sexuality* (Harvard University Press), "Kids are engaged with their sexuality at younger ages, but they're not necessarily sexually active. The good-girl, bad-girl thing has grown much more complicated." Did you know this? Don't shoot the messenger!

TV OR NOT TV (MORE SHAKESPEARE)

THAT FESTERING REMOTE-CONTROLLED STINKHOLE CAN BE

your friend, but, alas, poor television has become the most demonized medium in history.

Author-guys from the old days didn't have to compete with cartoons and never had to explain *Hung* or *The Real Housewives of New Jersey* to their kids. Whereas previous generations were introduced to media through print, this generation's pathway is electronic.

The American Academy of Pediatrics says parents should not let infants watch television, yet 25 percent of children under two have a TV in their bedrooms. Nielsen Media already tracks TV viewing by children that young, which is why *Sesame Street* has reconstructed its programs to make them easier to follow for younger children. Preschoolers spend two hours a day watching TV, videos, and computer screens, compared to forty minutes a day reading or being read to. Nearly all children under six have clothes or toys based on characters from TV shows or movies. DVDs are used by daycare centers to relax toddlers before their naps, and many stores provide monitors so children can watch videos in their strollers while Mom shops for that handbag.

The general consensus is that, properly supervised, TV can be a useful tool for social and educational development.

TV ROLE MODELS

YOU KNEW I'D SPEND SOME TIME TALKING ABOUT THAT ALL-TIME classic, *Growing Pains*, so here it goes. The Seavers were the Osbournes on Prozac. The lovely Joanna Kerns played my wife, and I'm happy to recall that I was one of the most popular TV dads in history, based on an actual survey conducted among those members of my immediate family listed on my tax form as "dependents."

We were proud of what our show stood for and of the kind of parents we tried to be. The show has never been off the air, even though we stopped taping in 1991, and they simply—and literally—don't make 'em like that anymore. Surveys in the early '90s showed that most American homes had two television sets—one for the adults and one for the kids. Consequently, shows for the family to watch together were no longer seen as necessary or profitable, and networks began concentrating on making one program for the kids and another for the grown-ups. The rerun beneficiaries were those shows that exemplified the best of the breed: *Growing Pains, Full House, The Cosby Show, Family Ties, Who's the Boss?*, and the like. It's easy to be cynical about those somewhat corny, simplistic chestnuts, but the world would be a kinder, gentler place if more of us behaved like those characters.

THE CURSE OF CNN

WE USED TO PLAY COWBOYS, BUT AFTER 9/11, I FOUND CARTER wanting to play Osama bin Laden. This was clearly unacceptable, and when he asked if he and his friends could play Hitler, I knew it was time to fill in the blanks left by the History Channel and explain the difference between low-grade bad guys—Jesse James and Billy the Kid come to mind—and the legendary reprehensibles of all time. Even the most nobly intended educational channels, which also include A&E, the Biography Channel, and Animal Planet, have to be monitored and tempered with some guidance and interpretation.

LARRY KING FRIGHTENS CHILDREN

KIDS ABSORB ANXIETY FROM SNIPPETS OF ADULT CONVERSATION and television news. My brother, Todd, chose to shelter his son, and Todd has parented to perfection because Evan's a gem. I took the other tack with Carter, knowing he would be exposed to unsavory words, ideas, and games within the first twenty minutes of preschool, so why not try to control what he would experience by taking charge?

Both methods can work in the long run, provided you stay on your game. Is he frightened by guns or too fond of them? Curious about the human body or shy about his own? Disapproving of bad words or interested in repeating them? Repulsed by classroom troublemakers or inclined to join them?

FEAR FACTOR

IN HER ARTICLE IN *TIME* MAGAZINE ON FEBRUARY 24, 2003, Claudia Wallis opined on how to manage kids' anxiety:

"Parents should keep their own fears out of the conversation. Answer their questions briefly, reassuringly, and without excessive detail. The amount of elaboration depends on the child's age and level of curiosity. If a five-year-old asks, 'Why are you buying that duct tape?' it may be enough to answer, 'It's a handy thing to have around.'"

How you talk to an eight-year-old about issues is very different from how you talk to a fourteen-year-old. "Too much information" is unnecessary and may confuse or scare a young child.

THE CHAIN OF PAIN

BE CAREFUL HOW MUCH YOU CHANGE YOUR LIFESTYLE OR THE tone of your household when a family member gets sick. Children are especially sensitive to unspoken grief, so think about how to talk to them about debilitating illness and, ultimately, death itself. Mystery and secrecy can frighten and disturb them more than a condensed version of the truth and an invitation to be in the loop. I was ten years old when my mother experienced complications from the birth of my younger brother. Dad was suddenly taking me to the movies so often that I knew something was up with Mom. On the plus side, I got to see a lifetime quota of Danny Kaye and Jerry Lewis films; on the downside, I was becoming aware that

I could be losing my mother. Dad fed me as much news as he thought I could handle, until, fortunately, Mom pulled through and we enjoyed many more healthy years together.

CUSSING: WHEN BAD WORDS HAPPEN TO GOOD PEOPLE

MY MOST SHOCKING RECOLLECTION OF THE F-WORD WAS WHEN it was spoken by, of all people, my grandfather, Willis, the kindest, most mild-mannered and gentle fellow imaginable—or at least that was the side he showed his grandson. I was an eleven-year-old doing my summer job at the car lot Will owned when I heard him rip into a loud, aggressive harangue, clearly upset at something an employee had mishandled and blaspheming almost aerobically at the offender. My job was to clean out the toilets in the restrooms, and it occurred to me I should be taking the mop and scrubbing out Will's mouth. I hadn't heard "that word" often, and certainly never as a noun, adjective, and adverb all in one sentence, but I knew instinctively that this would be the wrong time to ask him what it actually meant.

At the age of twelve, I was riding my bike with a new friend, having just moved to Ottawa from Hamilton to begin the seventh grade. As we puffed uphill, I remember being reluctant to initiate a conversation I had been anxious to have for some time: the meaning of the F-word. I still had no clue and wanted to ask someone who seemed precocious enough to have a reliable answer to this burning question because I was sure it involved a world I wanted to be part of. Paul Jennings seemed like he'd be that kind of guy...good athlete, girls liked him, he liked girls—all in all, a good bet to be my fountain of knowledge. Halfway up the hill, I summoned the nerve and breathlessly blurted, "Hey, by the way, what does **** mean around here? I know what it meant at my old school, but what does it mean when you guys say it?" I thought that was a clever way to disguise my innocence. And then he told me. Then I fell off my bike into the ditch. I wondered to myself, "Why would anybody want to do that?" It would be years before I would find out.

"WHERE DO THEY HEAR THIS STUFF?"

BESIDES GRANDFATHERS, THE ANSWER IS, UNFORTUNATELY, everywhere. Try to position yourself to be the one who sets the record straight.

SIBLINGNESS

BROTHERS AND SISTERS CAN, BY PROXY, EXERT YOUR INFLUENCE as a parent on one another—especially the older to the younger, with your firstborn being the flesh-and-blood proof of your excellence at parenting, a chance to see how you did the first time around. As the manipulative older one, I used to make my brother and sister compete to see who could make my bed faster. The winner got to get me a Coke.

RAISING KIDS THE RATTRAY WAY: A MULTI-GENDER SIBLING ESSAY FROM MY SISTER AND HER HUSBAND (BECAUSE THEY HAVE A BOY AND A GIRL AND I DON'T)

"HAVING ONE OF EACH REALLY SHOWS THE BUILT-IN CONTRAST that Mother Nature has provided. Victoria is interested in every fashion and fad and very particular about details—she even cries if there's too much brown sugar on her oatmeal in the morning. Creighton comes home with his pants on backwards and one sock in his pocket. He will wear a purple shirt with green pants, and his favorite color is orange. He doesn't complain about anything except his sister.

We try to guide each child along his or her special path, and we feel good about our efforts every night when, as they go to sleep, they remind us, 'Mom, Dad, I love you.'"

– Terry & Joanne Thicke-Rattray

ANIMAL INSTINCTS

DISNEY SET THE STANDARD FOR TEACHING HUMAN VALUES through anthropomorphism—a word I learned in college that I've waited all these years to use.

Psychologists believe that the early stages of morality can be taught through your child's love of animals, since caring for someone or something other than ourselves is the first sign of moral maturation. The child also comes to realize that behavior, which hurts another living thing is wrong.

Animal Planet is good to watch as long as you're prepared to explain the aforementioned "Circle of Life." You may not sing as well as Sir Elton, but anyone can play a DVD and point out that lions get hungry, too, even though it might be sad when lunch is that beautiful baby antelope or some unsuspecting wildebeest.

THE PROBLEM WITH HORSES

I FIRST BECAME AWARE THAT THE UNIVERSE WAS NOT ENTIRELY about me at age six, when my grandparents bought me a pony, thus solidifying their image as the coolest people on earth, notwithstanding Will's one incident of potty-mouth. As was our custom, we would be spending the summer at the family cottage a mile off the highway down a single-lane country road near Kirkland Lake. The pony's name was Blackie—a curious choice since he was a dapple gray color—but not being one to look a gift pony in the mouth, I accepted this incredible gift with open arms. My first month aboard Blackie was without incident, except for the time I tried to cowboy over to the neighbors' against my grandfather Will's will. He was worried that some tree-clearing was taking place next door and that any sudden noise by the workers might cause the pony to bolt, throwing me to the ground. Sure enough, as I ventured over to show off my steed, some idiot lumberjack did exactly what he got paid to do and started up his chainsaw. Blackie wasted no time rearing back and bolting, as predicted, scared-pony style, back to our cottage in what surely seemed like a gallop to a six-year-old.

Having survived with only a scolding and a warning, Blackie and I got a reprieve, until one day I was driving with Will and we spotted a bear at the side of the road. This was a thrill for me, but Willie the Wise made the connection between the hungry bear and the tied-up pony and immediately decided that his largely exposed makeshift barn was no place for Blackie and that he would be better off in a new home. Although I understood the danger, giving up my pony was a difficult, tear-filled concept to grasp, but I was ultimately able to put Blackie's welfare ahead of my own happiness, which, in retrospect, may be the nicest thing I've ever done.

THE "OLD MCDONALD HAD A FARM" ISSUE

YOUR KIDS CAN LEARN ABOUT CARING FOR THE WELFARE OF others by simple exercises such as taking them to the grocery store.

Some conscientious shoppers look for the "cage-free" sign on chickens, yet only 1 percent of all chickens are raised in a cage-free environment.

McDonald's has responded to consumer pressure by revising the way they raise their birds. It used to be that the little cluckers were kept nine to a cage, but they now live in the luxury of seven to a cage and have room to flap their wings. This seems like a modest improvement, but try telling that to a chicken whose only benefit is a little alone time for a few extra wing flaps before becoming your McNugget.

WHEN GROWN-UPS GO BAD: STUPID ADULTS EXPOSED

DON'T SET BAD EXAMPLES BY DOING ANNOYING THINGS—THE flip side of role modeling. I don't like the buffet morons who get their croutons one at a time...or the overhead compartment stuffers who slow things down in the airplane aisles by trying to wrestle their oversized "hand-carry" items into impossibly undersized spaces, jamming and probing against all known laws of physics and matter. Placing these people on a "no fly" list would alleviate "ramp chaos," a phenomenon in which 140 passengers are backed up and suffocating in a sweltering (or freezing cold) holding pen called a Jetway. But am I bitter? Yes. Their next seat should be an electric chair. Perhaps I've been too harsh.

Don't let your children pattern themselves after these unaware, self-absorbed oblivians. (Yes, I made up that word, as my spell-checker let me know.) You will be setting a bad language example yourself if you are inclined to cuss within earshot. Sound like you? Then stop it!

And why do people say "at this point in time"? Do you just like to hear yourself prattle on? "At this time" would cover it. "Now" is good. What the heck is a "point" in time? You don't say, "Excuse me, but do you have the point in time?" It's pretentious and not even syntactically correct. Stop it!

Sorry.

The other thing that bugs me is the opinion polls that *TIME* Magazine, CNN, and ESPN conduct to get Americans' advice about things. I understand polls that monitor voting trends, such as which Republican candidate we'll nominate to be pulverized in the next election. And I understand holding referendum on important issues like going to war, legalizing marijuana, and making it a capital crime to stuff an oversized bag into a 747's overhead compartment. But when they start asking, "Do you think we have enough bird flu vaccine?" does it really matter what you and I think? What the hell do we know? There are highly paid professionals whose opinions mean something—let's poll them. I can't be swayed by what a sitcom star or grocery store bagger thinks about the number of flu shots available. There's a good chance he'll be wrong, which, come to think of it, would make him a perfect candidate for government.

HIGHER STAKES

IT STARTS INNOCENTLY ENOUGH WITH FASHION AND FADS, BUT the pressure your child will face from his mates is bound to become more ominous, with sex, alcohol, and drugs on the horizon. Remember: dee-fense! Stay in the loop and stay ahead of the curve, and you'll be fine.

Education

"Does He Seem Slow to You?"

"The function of education is to teach one to think intensively and to think critically. Intelligence plus character—that is the goal of true education."

– Martin Luther King Jr.

LANGUAGE

YOU ARE WHERE EDUCATION BEGINS. KIDS WILL ABSORB everything you say and do, so stay lean on the baby talk: the baby is learning, and you are stunting his intellectual growth by spouting gibberish. "Use your words!" you'll often tell him. The same applies to you.

FIRST WORDS

MOST BABIES LEARN TO WALK AND TALK SIMULTANEOUSLY between twelve and fourteen months. Make it a point to point, and as you do, name familiar things like teddy bear, block, rattle, sock, jersey, and diaper. When familiar people visit, call them by name. When total strangers visit, call the police. Your baby will listen to you because what you say is stimulating. If only the rest of the world felt that way.

TOUGH QUESTIONS

"WHAT SHOULD I DO WHEN THEY ASK QUESTIONS I DON'T know the answers to?"

My solution would be to lie. Really. Make stuff up, because you must always appear knowledgeable. "How can you throw a ball and have it curve? Why do you get dizzy? Why is the sky blue and the ocean green? What is it like in heaven?"

Once you run out of creative answers for these questions, Google and Wikipedia are your friends.

HOMESCHOOLING

AGAIN, YOU'VE BEEN DOING IT SINCE DAY ONE. THINK OF YOUR home as "pre-preschool." One way to make learning fun is to invent your own games. Word games are handy, since you can play them anytime and anywhere, including in an automobile or after the lights are out when you're tucking him in—and they don't involve balls or Frisbees or swords or anything that could take out a costly lamp.

KNOCKOUT

TWO OF THESE LIVE IN THE OCEAN. KNOCK OUT THE ONE THAT does not:

Whale ... shark ... zebra.

Two of these were presidents. Knock out the one who was not.

Kennedy ... Clinton ... Gore.

I'm guessing you got the animal question right. Notwithstanding that strange balloting procedure in Florida, you probably got the second one right as well. If you got both of the above correct, you are smart enough to play Knockout with your five-year-old. If you scored one or worse, go ahead—pick up a bat and break the lamp.

Carter and I also enjoyed the Sentence Game, in which you have to make a sentence out of three unrelated words (e.g., pilot, dinosaur, and corn flakes). The sentences seldom made sense, but thinking in terms of grammatical composition it is a useful exercise, one that I believe contributed to Carter's ability to write full sentences in the first grade. Please note that these gems are copyrighted in my own mind. If you end up developing them with the Game Show Network into a series starring Tom Bergeron, I expect to be compensated with a royalty and profit participation.

HOMEWORK

CHOOSE ONE OF THE FOLLOWING:

a) Let them decide when to do their homework, where to do it, and how much to do.
b) Tell them to relax. The dog will eat it anyway.
c) When your child does homework, engage in a parallel activity. If your child is reading, you read, too. If he's doing math, balance your checkbook. Your child needs to see that the skills he is practicing are related to things you do as an adult.

If you chose c, you're off on the right foot. Homework is the source of more squabbles between schools and families than any other single topic. Students today come home with far more homework than their parents ever did, and they start much younger. That puts pressure on moms and dads, who are seldom told their proper role in homework. Should they be teacher, enforcer, or bystander?

From Harris Cooper, *The Battle over Homework* (Corwin Press):

1. Watch your child for indications of failure and frustration. If your child asks for help, provide guidance and clues but not answers. If frustration sets in, suggest a short break.
2. Set a schedule for when homework will be done.
3. Create an environment for children to do their work in a quiet, well-lighted place. Make sure the needed materials (paper, pencils, etc.) are available.
4. Schedule ten minutes of homework per night per grade—so that first-graders get ten minutes, second-graders twenty minutes, and so on. [Thicke note: Mr. Cooper's kids are getting off easy! Many schools will start with twenty or even thirty minutes in the first grade.]
5. Be a cheerleader. Homework provides an opportunity to tell your child how important school is. Be positive about homework and make it fun—but not too much. In addition to the math and reading, he's learning about accomplishment here and the attitude you express will be the attitude your child acquires.

I'd like to add, "Don't take their word for it." When Robin and Brennan were studying in their rooms, I would poke my head in and ask whether it was going well and whether they needed help. I admit it was a half-hearted token gesture on my part—I was actually afraid they might want help, in which case I'd be useless, since I was way out of the education loop by then. Although they always declined, things were not always going well, as I would learn weeks later at report card time. Signing a daily worksheet sent home by the teacher is a good idea. Ask the teacher to provide this if your school does not already offer this service.

TOO MUCH TOO SOON?

DECISIONS ABOUT EDUCATION ARE AMONG THE MOST CRITICAL choices you will ever make. It was only a generation ago that educationists considered individual curricula the preferred method. They had concluded that children should be brought along at their own speed, which made a lot of sense to parents of particularly bright children, who risked becoming bored if the program moved too slowly. Similarly, parents of slower children were concerned that theirs were being left behind. Meanwhile, many kids were being screwed up by homeschooling, in where the parents doing the schooling weren't the brightest bulbs on the tree themselves. Current thinking has shifted the pendulum back to the middle in terms of standardized rates of progress.

STATS ABOUT SATS

YOU PROBABLY KNOW THAT IQ TESTS PROBE INNATE INTELLIGENCE and general reasoning abilities, whereas SATs evaluate learned knowledge. SATs, however, were a foreign concept to me, because I was a foreigner. In my high school years in Ontario, we didn't even have "freshmen, sophomores, juniors, and seniors." Instead, we attended "grade 9, grade 10," and so on, up to grade 13—in fact, the Canadian equivalent of a college freshman. That meant students spending an extra year at home before college. How would that work for you and yours, delaying your empty nest and their freedom? Our grade 13 final exams were standardized throughout our province, so we all studied the same curriculum and had to know the same stuff, no matter where we attended school. There is currently a strong movement afoot for a standardized curriculum throughout the United States, a welcome trend for those of us who believe in structure. No child will be stifled by conforming to a system, because the clever child will find his way out of the box and above the pack. I was delighted to enroll my child in a school that emphasizes academics, requires uniforms, and subjugates individual expression to the greater good of the whole. Once that greater good is accomplished and the group needs are met, the individual can be encouraged to blossom.

BIG SAT FALLACY

"HOW WELL YOU DO ON THE SAT WILL DETERMINE HOW WELL you do in life." In fact, studies show that SAT scores have little power to predict earnings. Whew!

IF YOUR KID SCREWS UP, MOVE

PARENTS LIKE TO ENROLL THEIR KIDS IN SCHOOLS THAT include K-12 so they won't need to find another school; after all, just getting into the first one was a chore. However, let's look at this from another perspective: We've agreed that popularity is high on a student's list of priorities. With that in mind, consider that a change of schools gives kids an opportunity to reinvent themselves. First and second grade in Kansas, for example, teaches them what works about their own personalities compared to what works for others. Now, if they switch to St. Louis for the third grade, they'll have a chance to tweak their own behavior and brag about—and even exaggerate—what they were good at in the previous school. By ninth grade in, let's say, San Diego—Mom and Dad are into sailing—the kids might embellish their resumes further, and they'll have to live up to their new claims of grandeur. In the stories I told, I went from roadie to rockstar, from lip-synching as a backstage hanger-on to catching panties at the mike. Others I've met, although they were likely ski bums back home, made themselves sound like Olympic medalists when spinning their tales in their new locale. Such reinvention should not be in the "extreme makeover" category; it should involve less outright lying than exaggeration. If you want to be known as a champion equestrian, at least make sure you're not allergic to hay. The White House would call it "spin." An actor would call it a bio. If a little revisionist history benefits the "visualization/manifestation" process, maybe it's not such a bad thing.

SCHOOL ABSENCE

ARE YOU STRICT ENOUGH ABOUT TRUANCY? SOME SCHOOLS HAVE asked parents to voluntarily reimburse the school for state funds lost when a child misses school—about $40 per student per day.

CAREERS YOU NEED TO STAY IN SCHOOL TO STUDY FOR

YOUTH SURVEY SAYS BOYS THIRTEEN TO SEVENTEEN COMMONLY choose careers of doctor, lawyer, computer specialist, and professional athlete, while girls of that age choose doctor, teacher, and veterinarian. Careers that have fallen off the Gallup list in recent years include beautician, secretary, and flight attendant for girls; mechanic, electrician, and truck driver for boys. The reason given most often by kids for their preference is "to make a difference."

In an article by Barbara Kiviat called "The Partnership Glass

Ceiling," she states, "The number of female and minority legal professionals jumped significantly over the past three decades, but many remain in junior positions, with white males still running most major law firms, according to a study by the U.S. Equal Employment Opportunity Commission." She also says, "Women now account for 40 percent of legal professionals, compared with just 14 percent in 1975. Over that time period, the number of African Americans doubled, to 4 percent, and the number of Hispanics quadrupled, to 3 percent." The study concluded that among large firms, equal promotion is now more important than equal hiring.

PEACE AND THE FEMALE TOUCH

WE ARE ENLARGED AS A SPECIES WHEN GLASS CEILINGS ARE broken and women have as many choices as men. Queen Noor of Jordan—born Lisa Najeeb Halaby in New York to a wealthy Pan Am Airways exec of Arabic descent—believes women are key to peace-building efforts in the Middle East: "Women are left to pick up the shattered pieces of society when a conflict is over. If peace is truly to take place in the Middle East, women must play a role…the positions of women are the best indicators of a country's development."

A DOSE OF FINE ARTS

DON'T UNDERESTIMATE THE IMPORTANCE OF BALANCE IN YOUR child's education. Many medical schools now offer humanities coursework—novels, paintings, dance, and theater—alongside such staples as molecular biology and neuroscience. The theory behind this trend is that medical practitioners should connect with patients on a more spiritual and emotional level, rather than treating them as a mere collection of symptoms. At UC Irvine, anatomy students write essays about their cadavers, imagining who they were in life, before taking them apart.

TALK THE TALK

SADLY, AS A PRODUCT OF OUR EDUCATION SYSTEM, SOCIETY HAS lowered the bar in the area of literate, artful prose. John H. McWhorter writes the following in the *L.A. Times*:

"We don't hear eloquent speeches laying out nuanced positions with rhetorical finesse. Whatever happened to thoughtful, burnished language carefully crafted to sway those of other minds?

"The Gettysburg Address was a masterpiece of conciseness and persuasiveness when ordinary people loved their language in a way that is foreign to us now.

"This eloquence lasted into the 1960s, when John F. Kennedy spoke instead of talked. 'It is one of the ironies of our time,' he said in his State of the Union address, 'that the techniques of a harsh and repressive system should be able to instill discipline and ardor in its servants while the blessings of liberty have too often stood for privilege, materialism and a life of ease.' No current American public figure could venture communication pitched this high and expect to remain in office. Compare Kennedy's language to President Bush's four decades later: 'Bring it on. We have our marching orders. Let's roll.' Cute, but different. If Lincoln had ended his address with 'let's roll,' he might well have been assassinated two years earlier. Surely our leaders could do better. Jesse Jackson is an orator but in language that manipulates with short sentences and punchy rhythms. Carefully constructed rhetoric is against the cultural grain and instead we get quick hits on talk shows. In an America where to dress language up too far beyond the everyday is considered a gaffe, the recreationally contentious sound bite culture will remain the order of the day."

SCHOOL OF THE WORLD: OUR SUMMER AT DACHAU

IN THE NAME OF EXPANDING HORIZONS, I ARRANGED TO TAKE Brennan on a tour of Europe at the age of fourteen for his summer getaway. We strolled the boulevards of Paris and watched fashion models flutter by in the cafes of Milan. We visited cheese factories in Holland and marveled at the flowers in bloom in the Dutch countryside.

Our next stop was Amsterdam, where the big challenge was to keep the drug dealers and pimps far enough away so that Brennan didn't have to ask, "Who are these people?" Aiming higher, we visited the Anne Frank House, a museum that touched Brennan in a profound way. Encouraged by that show of sensitivity, on our next stop, in Frankfurt, Germany, I decided to push further and came up with the bright idea to visit the infamous Nazi concentration camp at Dachau. I thought that taking the train there, possibly traversing the very route once taken by doomed souls in those horrific days, would be a spiritual experience, but my German was somewhat lacking and I misread the rail schedule. After the taxi dropped us off at the train station, we sat for some time before noticing that we were the only passengers there. In fact, there would be no train that day. On that hot Teutonic afternoon—at least the weather was better than in Belgium—we set out on foot, hoping we were walking in the direction of the memorial. I was right about the direction but woefully wrong about the distance.

We walked for miles before Brennan started cussing. The practice was frowned on in our house, but under the circumstances I had to cut him a little slack. By the end of the second hour, my son began making threatening gestures. Once again, I allowed him some rope, believing that he wouldn't actually strike me. Three kilometers later he was questioning whether I was really his father. As sensitive as Brennan was to the Holocaust, he was not happy about walking five miles to a concentration camp while his friends were surfing Malibu. We consoled ourselves by agreeing that most of our trips over the following years would be to places you could drive to in the good old U. S. of A.

Money

"Honey, I Shrunk the Cash"

I'D LIKE TO TAKE YOU BACK TO CHAPTER 1, ITEM NUMBER 1 ON our "shortcut" list of How to Raise Kids Who Won't Hate You: "Buy their love." Everything they want. Lots of toys. Over and out.

In days of yore, people could actually make money by having kids who would till the fields and swing the blacksmith's anvil. When was the last time your son thatched a roof or your daughter ground wheat into flour? The concept of having a child to put your family finances in the black is unimaginable to most of us, but for those who doubt that you can make a profit on your kids, I give you two words: Olsen twins. These babes are a cash magnet! Not all children offer this kind of appreciation on your investment; in fact, kids and appreciation are two words seldom used in the same sentence. If there is any profit to be gained, it is social rather than material—the interpersonal networks kids create among parent auxiliary groups, soccer moms, T-ball dads, and the like. Our children become a means of meeting other adults, some of whom become our good friends while others just piss us off when they point out how much better their child is doing at spelling or karate. You may even make acquaintances in your field of work and discover that your kids have provided you with a human business card.

"MOMMY, WHY ARE THEY RICHER THAN US?"

"WELL, SWEETIE, I MARRIED A LOSER. YOUR DAD WASN'T VERY bright…or ambitious. In fact, in college he was such an underachiever…"

This doesn't apply to you, of course, but be prepared when your child notices that his classmate—Trump Junior—has more stuff. Remember the "money isn't everything" speech your dad gave you?

THE BEST ADVICE I EVER GAVE MY KIDS ON MONEY MATTERS

"THE DIFFERENCE BETWEEN A GOOD IDEA AND A DOLLAR IS 99 cents." You can use this if you like. Effort and tenacity have to go hand in hand with genius when it comes to forging a career and making a living.

HARLEY ISN'T THE ONLY HOG AROUND HERE

IF YOU UNDERSTAND OUR MISSION BY NOW, IT IS TO TURN OUT kids who are better than us and will accomplish things we never could. Maybe your son will play in the bigs or your daughter will be chief of medicine at Harvard, whereas you couldn't lay down a bunt or diagnose a cold sore.

With those long-range goals in mind, we supply our little ones with bats and balls and toy stethoscopes, underscoring our own fascination with pro sports and science and our hope that they'll get hooked on something that might generate revenue one day so they can buy expensive toys for themselves.

I bought Brennan a Honda motorbike for his fourteenth birthday (atoning for Dachau?), knowing fully that he could not legally drive it until his sixteenth birthday. I figured he could have a little fun tooling around on our few acres of ranch property, up and down the driveway. Boy, was I wrong! What fourteen-year-old wants to go up and down the driveway only? This was a big tease, a pork chop dangled just out of a pit bull's reach. Dads, don't just get them trains you want to play with or remote control cars you want to drive. They'll catch on and you won't look quite so generous.

It served me right when years later Brennan became an authentic Harley rider, a borderline Hells Angel. He developed a very pricey taste for the most powerful and loudest motorcycles on the planet, all of which somehow ended up on my vehicle insurance tab. The payoff came during a recent bonding adventure at a Hells Angels ride, which culminated in a tattoo contest with me as the honorary judge. I'm not kidding. I was invited to examine tattoos on body parts that only doctors should visit, and I was genuinely impressed, even amazed, at what I learned about recent breakthroughs in the tattoo industry. One guy had Elvis emblazoned on his chest and could make the King's lip quiver with a flick of his pec. Outstanding. One girl had an image of Jesus in one of the last places you would expect to find Jesus.

Two girls, whose jeans were slung so low a plumber would be embarrassed, scurried over to introduce themselves, gushing about how they had grown up watching *Growing Pains* and how I had, in some fashion, raised them. Pointing to my son, I said, "Well, then, say hello to your brother Brennan." The girls giggled, and Brennan was able to strike up a conversation that led who knows where and to who knows what, but it seemed to go well. Meanwhile, I was still tooling around town doing errands on that minibike, looking for all the world like a middle-aged helmeted Snoopy on wheels.

INSURANCE ASSURANCE

YOU WILL FIND, AS I DID IN THE FAILED "BIKE-ON-HOLD" SCHEME, that kids have short attention spans and will have trouble understanding a payoff that doesn't come until years down the road. They don't get "mortality," because they're invincible. You can try talking to your adolescents about the fact that you are tapped out because you are paying for a life insurance policy that will care for them in the instance of your death, but even dutiful offspring will acknowledge that gesture and accept that explanation for only several seconds before asking if you managed to get tickets to the Lakers game Saturday night. (Clippers tickets were available.)

GEM FACTOID

A company called Lifegem can transform your ashes into precious diamonds for your loved ones at a cost of about $2,100 for a quarter-karat. There's enough carbon in a corpse to make fifty diamonds. Diamonds are a stiff's best friend.

WHERE THERE'S A WILL, THERE'S A WAY...TOO MANY RELATIVES

LATER IN THEIR TEENS, YOUR KIDS MAY FINALLY BECOME rightfully curious about how much life insurance you have. As they contemplate their own futures and occupations, it will be to their advantage to know whether they're going to get rich or get stiffed. Without going into the details, give them a ballpark idea. When selecting her "career," it probably didn't hurt Paris Hilton to know that she owns hotels around the world. A kid applying for college might go with his heart and choose a more socially conscious pursuit, such as teaching, if he has assurance of insurance—a few bucks from you that could kick in down the road. Let the child know what he can expect in terms of college tuition, a car, an allowance, and a house.

Encourage them to balance following their passions and following the money train if there seems to be any conflict between the two. From my experience, I would not recommend showbiz to anyone not born into a wealthy family. Some kids write screenplays and tend bar well into their forties for the simple reason that entertainment is not a fair or just business. After *Thicke of the Night* was canceled and I got another shot at the brass ring with *Growing Pains*, I determined that even though my acquaintances were many, I could count my true friends on one hand. I could account for the others on one finger—yes, that one. I decided that if I got another opportunity, I would sell out as quickly and thoroughly as possible, grabbing every parade, beauty pageant, awards presentation, dog show, commercial, infomercial, mall opening, and autograph signing as long as there was cash involved. I also did plenty of charity work, so I'm not concerned about going to heaven on that score. My career decision, however, was to make sure "they" could never take it all away from me again, that I would be able to provide for my children and that we would be secure as a family. By selling out, I was able to fulfill that promise and make my children's transition to adulthood a little easier. I'm at peace with that decision and would make it again 100 times out of 100. Holding out for that Oscar role and the elusive artistic credibility that show business so subjectively offers—and then offers to someone else next year—is a cautionary tale, to be sure.

At my house, we have a Shrine of Gratitude to Warner Brothers and the Nielsen families that we bow to on special occasions.

THOSE OLSENS AND BEYOND

MARY-KATE AND ASHLEY HAVE A FORTUNE ESTIMATED AT $150 million each. Their empire has grossed as much as $1 billion in a single year, and no, you can't trade two of your kids for one of them.

Mary-Kate has acknowledged that she has attention deficit disorder, although with her discretionary income, anything might have a tough time holding her attention. "We don't go around partying and doing bad stuff that we could be caught for," Mary-Kate said, sounding like she wanted to party but not get caught. "In their younger days, they attended private parties at homes of friends and have been spotted nipping at hard liquor on occasion, but always discreetly. They'd pour vodka into water bottles and sip from those," said a friend—who doesn't sound like much of a friend.

Ashley and Mary-Kate always said they would wait until marriage to have sex, and four million boys waited anxiously along with them. I have no inside information as to how those laudable vows have held up, but I read the tabloids enough to know I should now have my doubts.

TRUMPING THE OLSENS

"I KNEW I WAS PRIVILEGED WHEN I VISITED OTHER KIDS' homes," says Donald Trump Jr. "I realized how fortunate I was coming home to a triplex in NYC's Trump Tower." About their allowance, Donald Sr. claims, "My kids often complained that compared to their friends', theirs was paltry." However, it's likely that The Donald's "paltry" is different from your "paltry."

If a junior Trump is looking for the girl-next-door type, look no further than Paris and Nicky Hilton, who were raised in the Waldorf-Astoria. As the great-granddaughters of hotel founder Conrad Hilton, these swell gals are heirs to the family's $5.2 billion fortune. "I didn't have any chores growing up," says Paris. "Oh, wait, I did have to walk my dog and make my bed." Sounds like child abuse to me.

Harry and William Windsor, the children of Prince Charles and Princess Diana, are in line for $30 million, which is a meager sum compared to the family fund of $10 billion. Maybe they're serving a time-out for drinking, dancing, and generally un-Olsen-like behavior. Nevertheless, one of them gets to be King of England one day, with time-shares in Canada and Australia. You can't offer your kid that.

Athina Onassis Roussel, granddaughter of Aristotle Onassis, got $800 million on her eighteenth birthday. Her nineteenth must have been anticlimactic.

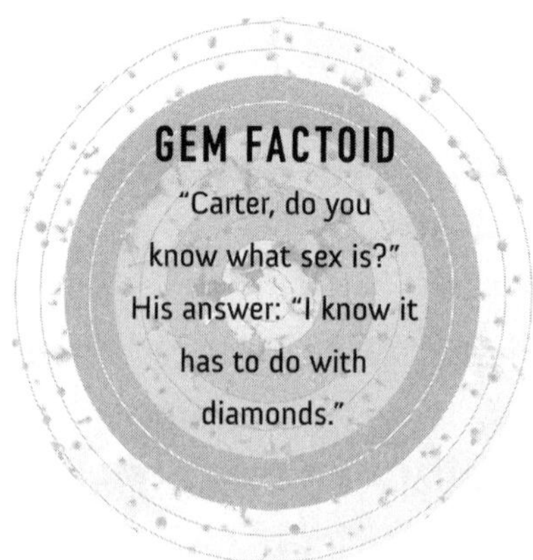

GEM FACTOID
"Carter, do you
know what sex is?"
His answer: "I know it
has to do with
diamonds."

Sports

When Daddy Throws Like a Girl

THE PLEASURE OF PLAYING ALONE—NOT TO BE CONFUSED with playing with yourself, which we cover in Chapter 14—has been documented by, you guessed it, Mr. Brott. While babies love to play with others, they are also content to play by themselves for short periods of time, so don't be afraid to let them go according to their whims and at their own pace. Because too much play can make your child fussy or irritable, limit sessions to around five minutes. When your baby cries or seems bored with you, take a hint and give it a rest before you become an annoyance.

Babies can also get bored with adults who talk too little or too much. They may be more fascinated with their hands and feet than they are with you. You could become second fiddle to a toe. If you want to be interesting to your child, be interested in what he's doing, but don't overdo it and prevent your child from learning on his own. Children who rely on their parents for stimulation may seem bored at daycare, when in reality they might simply lack curiosity and self-motivation.

Beanbags are fun and different because they don't roll. You knew this.

LE DIFFERENCE

FATHERS AND MOTHERS HAVE DISTINCT BUT COMPLEMENTARY styles of playing with their children. While dads tend to be more physical, encouraging kids to do things for themselves and take more risks, mothers tend to be more protective, sparing their children from disappointment whenever possible.

Example: If a kid is building a tower that is about to collapse, Dad will let it fall, whereas Mom will steady the tower as it teeters. You may call this meddling and prefer that they get ready for the real world of frustration, failure, rejection, bankruptcy, carjacking, and a lifetime of faulty towers.

THE TIME-TESTED THEORY OF BUILDING BLOCKS

THE OLD-FASHIONED, LOW-TECH, CHEAPEST THING GOING IS still an essential part of every nursery: building blocks. They develop hand-eye coordination and grasping and releasing skills, and they provide lessons in patterns, sizes, categories, gravity, balance, and structure. These elementary lessons in math and physics lay the foundation for your baby's understanding of how the world works. (Oh, that it would be so simple!)

Blocks teach thinking skills and perseverance: building a tower can be a frustrating experience—for any non-Trump. Even Albert Einstein opined, "Taken from a psychological viewpoint, this combinatory play of blocks and puzzles seems to be the essential feature in productive thought before there is any connection with logical construction in words or other kinds of signs which can be communicated to others." Mr. Einstein tended to ramble and might have had time for a decent haircut had he learned as much about editing as he did about blocks.

GENDER-SPECIFIC PLAY

ANYONE WHO BELIEVES IN GENDER EQUALITY HAS NEVER observed a play group of eighteen-month-olds. Girls are cats and boys are dogs. Girls do that coy, fuzzy kitten-like thing, while boys start panting and exhibiting senseless, over-the-top behavior, possibly a cause-and-effect dynamic.

WHY SPORTS ARE GOOD

"ONLY PUT YOUR CHILD IN A SITUATION IN WHICH THEY can be successful." (Consensus)

On the other hand: "Don't let what you cannot do interfere with what you can do." (John Wooden)

On achievement: "Winning is not a sometime thing; it's an all-time thing. You don't win once in a while; you don't do things right once in a while; you do them right all the time. Winning is a habit. Unfortunately, so is losing." (Vince Lombardi)

On effort: "The harder you work, the luckier you get." (Gary Player)

On courage: "What matters is not the size of the dog in the fight, but the size of the fight in the dog." (Bear Bryant)

On corny old sports metaphors: "Teach them to your kid, because they do make sense." (Me)

Carter didn't get the concept of parents cheering. I'd yell encouragement from the sidelines at soccer and he'd stop running, look over at me, and start to walk closer so he could hear me. "Get back out there," I'd say. "You have to listen with one ear and play at the same time." I can see how this might create anxiety in a kid who wants his Saturday to be fun and not a pressure cooker.

"Organized sports" is a misnomer if you've ever seen five-year-olds play soccer or T-ball. Sweet, but completely random. And although there's a quaint policy that no one keeps score, every kid (and their parents) will be able to tell you exactly how many goals his fabulous team had compared to their stinky opponents.

Alexander Wolff wrote an insightful report for *Sports Illustrated* in which he examined the American athlete at age ten. He identified a crossroads quality to being ten, by which time kids usually have a fully developed conscience—they'll say, "That's not fair," and they'll mean it.

Ten-year-olds love to be praised (do we ever grow out of that?). They like to be asked for their opinions and tell you what they know. They like to belong, whether it is to a club, a team, or a group. Ten-year-olds also like to hear true stories, not just made-up ones.

Sports, after all, offer many of the things ten-year-olds crave. Teams are clubs to which they can belong; victories and defeats are real, not make-believe; and rules are supposed to be applied evenly.

While eight- and nine-year-olds tend to be conformist, willing to try a wide range of things, ten-year-olds will assert their independence and delve more deeply into their passions. Sports will not exactly separate the men from the boys at this age, but it will separate the boys from the bigger boys according to size and skill level. However, the American Academy of Pediatrics opposes specialization before a child reaches puberty. A study by the Institute for the Study of Youth Sports concluded that the number-one reason ten-year-olds participate is "to have fun," rather than "the excitement of competition" or "to learn new skills." Kids who abandoned sports at ten were asked what might lure them back, and the top three answers were, "If practices were more fun," "If I could play more," and "If coaches understood players better."

By age thirteen, almost one-third of the kids who were active in sports as ten-year-olds will have dropped out. When coaches and parents take the fun out with misplaced emphasis and bad behavior, kids increasingly turn to the adult-free world of extreme sports, in which they can make their own rules.

"My advice to every ten-year-old baseball player is to put down your glove at the end of the season and try something else," says Cal Ripken Jr. Most experts agree that a child can be exposed to sports as late as ten and not be at a competitive disadvantage later—with one exception being tennis, where coaches believe it's worth "grooving the strokes" as early as five.

WHEN CAN WE PLAY TO WIN?

THE HALLS OF JUSTICE AND TABLOIDS ARE FILLED WITH STORIES of underachieving fathers with overambitious plans for their unenthusiastic children. Jennifer Capriati attributes her drug use and party life to rebellion against a strict father. Jelena Dokic had to put a restraining order on her coach/dad. Quarterback Todd Marinovich would still be calling signals for the Oakland Raiders if he could remember them. Unfortunately, his NFL career was cut short by marijuana abuse, possibly attributable in part to a father who groomed him from the age of four to be an NFL draft pick.

On the other hand, if children are motivated and enjoy a sport on their own terms, they will be more likely to reap their athletic potential. A proficiency in sports should be nurtured just as wholeheartedly as a penchant for music, art, or letters. You wouldn't discourage your whiz kid from memorizing math tables if that's what turns him on. Competitiveness is a good quality to have in the two-minute drills of real life, the characteristic known as "give me the ball at crunch time."

FACTOID PROFILE OF THE TEN-YEAR-OLD

I DON'T KNOW WHERE I GOT THIS NEXT STUFF, BECAUSE I lost my notes on this one. Sorry. Anyway, you ought to trust me by now.

- Favorite sports to play: (1) basketball, (2) football, (3) soccer
- Favorite sport to watch: baseball
- Percentage of kids who have stopped playing a sport because they lacked the time: 30
- Percentage of kids who own a Nintendo Wii, Sony PlayStation, or PSP: 60
- Percentage of kids with cell phones: 17
- Percentage of kids who think Pete Rose should be allowed in the Hall of Fame: 54
- Percentage of kids who believe having a boyfriend or girlfriend—or not—is the biggest difficulty facing them: 40

A ten-year-old boy is more likely to join a team first and then make friends among his teammates. Girls at ten tend to join teams with their preexisting friends.

A GOLDEN BEAR HUG

HERE'S A SPORTS ANECDOTE THAT HAS NOTHING TO DO WITH raising kids, except that I hope mine will read it one day.

Perhaps the most excited I've ever been with a man was when Jack Nicklaus pulled my name out of a hat, making me his partner in a pro-celebrity golf tournament. It was in La Quinta, California, 1994, and the small field could not have been more elite with Trevino, Chi-Chi, Palmer, Floyd, Stockton, Irwin, Costner, Smokey Robinson, and Dr. J.

The only Glory Day in my uneventful golf career came on a par-3 in that tournament, 200 yards over water. Mr. Nicklaus began by hitting his tee shot into the pond and looked at me as if to say, "If we score 5 on this hole, we're out of the tournament. What are you going to do about it?" I fearlessly reared back with my often-erratic 5-wood and smoked one onto the green, rolling up to the pin and missing the hole-in-one by a foot! I bowed and waved to a lot of people as we walked closer, prouder than a peacock with money, and proceeded to line up that putt, checking every angle and blade of grass, as well as the wind, the sun, and the stars. I asked anyone who'd listen—caddies, groundskeepers, spectators, total strangers, passersby, and a family of ducks—if they saw anything in the lay of the green that would aid my putt. "Does it move left or right?" Finally, a voice losing patience from the tee behind us yelled, "Hey, who's the putz who isn't putting?" It was Lee Trevino, and he meant me. I stroked the ball in for a 2 net 1, and Jack—I could call him that now—smiled and said, "You just earned yourself a set of clubs."

A week later, the FedEx man arrived at my door with a compete set of Jack Nicklaus golf clubs, all custom-made to my specs, in a gorgeous Jack Nicklaus golf bag.

One week after that, I boarded a plane for a tournament in Florida and checked my clubs. That was the last time I ever saw them. My guess is that a brand-new Nicklaus set was just too attractive to some golf-bitten baggage handler. I hope he never makes par again. (I won't mention the airline, but if it were a girl, her name would be Delta.)

THE PUCK STOPS HERE

WHEN CHOOSING A SPORT FOR YOUR SON OR DAUGHTER TO try, you could do a lot worse than the game of ice hockey. (Yes, women enjoy the heck out of the sport, too, and at the Olympics, they put on a great show.) There are many elements to commend in the sport, although many non-aficionados complain they can't follow the puck on television. Get over it! You don't always see the ball in a football game, because the ball-carriers are trying to hide it. If you were raised in these United States, however, you will have seen approximately two million hours of football and will therefore be familiar with the rhythm of the players on the field, allowing you to anticipate where the ball is going. Canadians have the same intuitive feeling about their pucks.

On the plus side, there are only two rules in hockey: Hit somebody over the head with your stick and you sit in the penalty box for two minutes. If he bleeds, you're there for five minutes. Other than that, sit back and enjoy a sport with the finesse of basketball, the body contact of football, and a speed rivaled only by NASCAR.

In terms of character building, there is a deep-rooted, time-honored culture in hockey that values humility, respect, tradition, and sportsmanship over egocentricity and trash-talking. Don't laugh—it's the only sport in which opposing players who've been knocking the snot out of each other in a playoff series will line up and shake hands when the battle is won. There's even a dress code: players who are scratched from the lineup due to injury or disfavor will attend that game in suits and ties, an arcane fashion tradition not seen in the bling-bling world of sports until recently. As combative and argumentative as hockey players are on the ice, that's how understated and warm they are off it.

OK, there are exceptions, but generally speaking, they exhibit enough testosterone in the game that they needn't prove themselves at the disco afterwards. Besides, hockey players are notoriously lousy dancers.

BLAME IT ON CANADA

MY PERSONAL THEORY IS THAT FOR DECADES, MOST HOCKEY PROS came from Canada—a land famous for its unimposing gentleness and humanity—and the game's traditions were established in that mold. Kids were identified as phenoms by their early teens and plucked from small towns in Saskatchewan and Quebec, then sent to bigger cities for more coaching and competition. Here they were often billeted with other families and had to be on their best behavior despite being lonesome much of the time, a wrenching experience for any fifteen-year-old.

Few professional players came from the college ranks, so they never received the coddling that the "big man on campus" does in the United States. With their bulky pants, they had none of the appeal of basketball players, who were taller and got to show their legs a lot, or football players, who were adored for their splendid buns. Hockey players would flash that "come hither" smile, but a toothless grin was seldom a turn-on. Where I came from, a guy was considered attractive if his stitches had healed; if his nose was still somewhere below his eyes and between his ears, he was considered a hunk. There's precious little room for conceit in that lifestyle.

Let's hope that with today's higher salaries and better dentistry, the pros don't lose sight of what has made them so appealing for generations.

WHY SOCCER SUCKS

I REALIZE I'VE JUST LOST MOST OF MY LATIN AUDIENCE, AND FOR the people who love the "game without hands," this book may be used for lighting the fire at your next weenie roast, where you wish I were the weenie. Please know that I am not impugning the merits of the world's most popular sport, but the American youth interest in soccer has never translated to a national adult passion for one simple reason: when American boys turn thirteen, they want to hit somebody!

I was once a spokesperson for AYSO (American Youth Soccer Organization) and happy to promote the virtues of the "sport without scoring" to the American public. I am pleased that my three sons enjoyed their leagues every weekend, and the only real beef I ever had about soccer was the parking: two thousand kids (with 4,000 parents) plus parking for fifteen cars equals a pain in the ass. (In L.A., that's 2,000 divorces…8,000 parents and stepparents, all accustomed to valet parking. It's a wonder there isn't more gunplay.)

AUNTIE BEANBALL

ESTABLISHING FAMILY SPORTS TRADITIONS IS A GREAT WAY to create history: touch football at Thanksgiving, a golf tournament on your birthday, the annual Christmas ice skating party, and the like. One side of my family was very competitive, so much so that the other side wouldn't play with them. The Jefferys were especially intense on the softball field and would seize any opportunity to get a game together with those family members who were still speaking to them. Family reunions meant a chance to play coed against our aging aunts, who regularly got the crap beaten out of them. These sweet little old ladies would show up in their deck sneakers knowing at least one would be injured per game—someone would either twist an ankle, get beaned by a brush-back pitch high and inside, or find herself on the business end of a hard slide into second base, spikes flying, boat shoes be damned. One particularly victimized aunt used to get even by making a really crummy meatloaf.

GOOD SPORTS

Robin, Young Jordan Fan

Robin, Still Lap-size

A-Rod and A-Bad Hair Day

"Hey, hey, Michael J., who's the blonde in Section A?"

Comparing anti-inflammatory prescriptions with Bobby Orr

"Thanks for the memories, Wayne.
Now get out of that sweaty jersey so we can dance!"

"That NHL lockout was a bummer!"

Sex

Find a Nice Place for Them to Have It (Of Course Not!)

FIRST LAW OF SEX

DON'T EVER LET THEM SEE YOU HAVING IT. YOU PROBABLY don't look that great doing it, and they wouldn't understand anyway. It usually looks like one of you is getting hurt and the other is out of control.

WHAT IS SEX? AND WHERE CAN I GET SOME?

LONG BEFORE YOU LOSE SLEEP OVER WHETHER YOUR BABY IS sexually active, you will be asked what sex is. Tell them it's grown-ups wrestling. Why do they sweat? They're wrestling really hard. Be ready to address this question as early as age four with a thoughtful, simple answer. You're on your own for the details.

"SPENCER JUST SHOWED ME HIS PENIS!"

OK, EVERYBODY, JUST CALM DOWN. WE'LL FIGURE THIS OUT AND deal with it.

If this happens, you'll feel guilty that you didn't supervise enough, forewarn enough. Somewhere in your child's life, there will be a Spencer who, for whatever reason, likes to whip out that tiny weapon at a moment's notice because he enjoys showing it to people. Very presidential.

So how do you react without scarring your baby for life? Teach them that private parts are private and that some rules must simply be obeyed. Children become aware of their sexual orientation as early as age ten—I purposely didn't mention that in the sports chapter—and young people spend their years of maximum sexual arousability in a society that bombards them with erotic images. It does no good to deny information to adolescents while they're in this state of "suspended sexuality."

Pundits complain that pop culture relentlessly pounds out the message that if you haven't had sex, you're a loser, and that sex appeal is the gold standard of human achievement and the coolest thing to aspire to. It's not just TV and the Internet and movies and music, but the billboards where bras are undone, pants are askew, and everyone has that look in their eye. Some parents turn their radio off while taking their kids to school because the shock jocks seem fixated on oral sex. (When I was a kid, oral sex was just talking about it.) The FCC is trying to stem the tide, but it's a big tide.

THE P WORD

IF YOUR CHILDREN DON'T RUN AWAY FROM HOME DURING puberty, you should. Move to Afghanistan—it's safer there.

SEAVER SEX

FAMILY SITCOMS THRIVE ON THE FACT THAT THERE IS NO KNOWN cure for puberty, and when those teens enter the TestosterZone, the parents become Pubo-Cops on Patrol.

Jason Seaver knew that teenage boys are hormones with feet and that when three guys go into their room and lock the door, the magazines come out. When heat starts emanating from your son's walls and steam flows from under the door, be prepared to call the paramedics to come and pump a Lady GaGa poster out of some kid's stomach.

It would be nice if our children could stay away from sex until they were old enough to feel the guilt and shame that go along with it. You may be one of those enviable parents whose child has chosen celibacy until marriage. For those unfamiliar with the term, celibate means "cranky."

SEX WITH FRIENDS

A SURVEY PUBLISHED IN THE JOURNAL *PEDIATRICS* IN 2003 focused on an episode of *Friends* in which Rachel discovers she is pregnant with Ross's child because of a broken condom. Twice during the episode, the characters say condoms are 97 percent effective. Among teens surveyed following the show, 65 percent remembered that the pregnancy involved a broken condom. Teens who watched the episode with a parent were twice as likely to correctly remember the actual statistics of condom effectiveness. Watch those reruns!

THE PRETTY DESK CLERK

MY COMING-OF-AGE EXPERIENCES INCLUDE ONE IN SANDUSKY, Ohio, in a cramped sports car where I was nearly put in permanent neutral by a stick shift in a failed "first-time" attempt. The moment was also highlighted by my frustration with a condom that came with no guidebook or diagrams. However, my most traumatic "close call" came in the summer of my sixteenth year, when my grandparents recruited me to drive them in their old Studebaker from Toronto to Edmonton, a distance of 2,000 miles. It didn't seem to bother them that I was underage and did not have a driver's license. Grandpa Steve Jeffery was a stocky bull of a man and a legendary cheapskate, a pensioner who never got rich as a hardware store operator, so when his vacation plan included a trip west to visit my dad, a driver working for minimum wage (or less) would be a practical addition, and thus I was invited along. His wife, Jean, was old and cantankerous, and their other companion, George, was older than both of them combined and told the same story every four hours. It was a good story, however, and that was important, since my grandfather had the only car in town without a radio, an optional expense, and we all knew which way Grandpa went with optional expenses. Our route took us across the northernmost fringes of Ontarian civilization: railroad stops named after some part of a moose, with one intersection, a beer parlor, two donut shops, and little else. Restaurant food can strain the budget, so we stopped at picnic tables and ate Jean's tomato-and-cheese sandwiches.

On our first night we checked into a hotel (or rather the hotel) in Hearst, Ontario—an eight-room two-story building from the mid-1800s—and I remember noticing that the young lady clerk behind the desk was flirting with me. That might have been wishful thinking, but knowing that my party would be asleep by 8 p.m., I asked whether there was anything happening in town that night. She told me about a wedding reception in the basement of the hotel that I could attend for $2. It seemed strange that one could buy a ticket for a wedding, but this was, after all, a town of only 1,500 people, and the bride and groom no doubt got a cut of the gate receipts, so God bless 'em. Come party time, the pretty desk clerk seemed to be alone and available for a chat. That I could have been seen as remotely seductive or interesting at the age of fifteen was some measure of how isolated the town of Hearst really was. We danced a little and I bought us each a beer—only fifteen but with the maturity of a twelve-year-old. Halfway through the beer I had become either chivalrous enough or randy enough to offer her an escort for the four-block walk home. She invited me into her apartment, a custom I would come to cherish over the years, and we started "necking," as we used to call it. I knew she meant business when she turned out the lights. It was either that, or my acne was becoming a deal breaker.

After a few minutes of wrestling on the sofa, I noticed I was perspiring—at least it felt like perspiration, because I could feel moisture on my lip. When the perspiration became a torrent, I turned on the lights and the two of us suddenly shrieked in horror. There was blood all over her face, and she saw blood spread over mine, and we ran to the bathroom to see what had happened. As it turned out, my untested libido had apparently made my nose bleed. This was a big buzz buster, and I was out of her apartment within minutes. I thought about describing the whole experience to my grandparents the next morning, but we had a cheese sandwich instead.

IS ANYBODY NORMAL HERE?

SOME KIDS WAIT UNTIL THEY'RE ADULTS TO HATE YOU, because they need scapegoats. ("Why didn't someone tell me?!") If sexuality plays a role in the self-esteem of an adolescent, it can absolutely define that of an adult. "For most people, what they think about themselves as a sexual person is a very important part of how they think about themselves as human beings," says John Bancroft, M.D., director of the Kinsey Institute.

No two people are exactly the same in their level of sexual interest or patterns of preference, and because of this variability, there is no such thing as "normal" frequency or a "normal" panoply of fantasies.

"What is right for two people in a relationship is what works for them," Bancroft says. In other words, the ostrich suit and the peanut butter are not out-of-bounds.

DISTURBING FACTOID

Most women do not achieve orgasm through intercourse alone. (I think I've dated them.) A Kinsey study found that the quality of women's emotional interaction during sex proved more important than the physical aspects, such as orgasm, in determining sexual satisfaction. (That makes me 0-for-2?)

TOO MUCH INFORMATION

PATROLLING CHILDREN IN YOUR NEIGHBORHOOD IS CHALLENGING enough without adding the infinite expanse of cyberspace to your domain—but you must! Luring children to Internet porn sites is a crime, as is knowingly using a misleading domain name to lead minors to harmful material (AMBER Alert legislation, 2003). One method is typo-squatting, in which sites are registered under subtly misspelled names of popular legitimate sites. Examples have included dinsneyland.com, teenmagzine.com, and britneyspeers.com.

Parental control services can be found at MSN 8.0, AOL Guardian, CyberPatrol, Pearl Software's Cyber Snoop, and SpectorSoft. Most can shut down access during specified hours (like 3 a.m.!) and provide weekly activity reports of where your children have surfed, as well as their e-mail and IM traffic (cost: approx. $40 annually). Discuss Internet safety with your kids. Teach them not to give out personal information (like their address or phone number) over the Internet. Their friends already know, and nobody else needs to.

In addition, parents should place time limits on Internet usage, restrict access to chat lines, and watch for warning flags that our children are being manipulated by offenders, including mysterious computer or telephone use and any clues that the child's home or school may be under unwelcome surveillance.

PORN YESTERDAY

KIDS DON'T INVENT SUGGESTIVE MATERIAL; THEY JUST FIND IT. When photography became widely available in the nineteenth century, it was soon put to use in providing stimulating images. More recently, the Internet has been both a boon and a menace to healthy sexuality. Although it can serve as a means of support and connection for those whose sexuality makes them feel isolated, others are unable to resist the lure of interactive Internet pornography.

Bancroft: "Because an extraordinary variety of sexual stimuli is accessible in relatively private settings, Internet erotica is potentially far more dangerous than traditional print or video sources and can interfere with relationships and work performance while emptying bank accounts." The National Council on Sex Addiction and Compulsivity estimates that a staggering two million people are addicted to cybersex.

CROSSING THE LINE

ACTRESS SUSAN DEY ("LAURIE" ON *THE PARTRIDGE FAMILY*) has volunteered at the rape treatment center in Santa Monica for fifteen years and offers the following unsettling statistics:

- Half of all rape victims are eighteen or younger.
- The rapists are acquaintances 80 percent of the time.
- In many cases, the victims are incapacitated by drugs or alcohol, and there are even cases where victims have been "tagged": the rapist will use a felt-tipped pen to mark his conquest just as a gang banger leaves his mark on a wall.

FEAR OF SEXUAL FEELINGS

THERE'S A WRITER I'VE ALREADY QUOTED WHO HAS A NOTION so controversial I will only paraphrase here.

He asks you to imagine you're rolling around on the floor with your baby and, without warning, you get "aroused." Surprisingly, the majority of mental health professionals say that it is normal for parents to experience fleeting sexual feelings toward their own children. These desires, brief as they might be, can be especially terrifying for men. You may want to have yourself locked up, thinking you're completely insane. If this urge hits you, get over the guilt before you withdraw from your child and stop playing with or cuddling her. Odds are you will never behave inappropriately, but if you think you need counseling, contact a professional. Don't call me—I'll just think you're a cuckoo.

MASTURBATION

WANNA SKIP THIS ONE AND JUST LIVE IN DENIAL?

Boys will start some form of masturbation as early as five years old, a frightening revelation to mothers who never had brothers and have no idea what they're getting themselves into. How to handle a masturbating five-year-old is a touchy question (pun intended). Does your place of worship offer guidelines? Let's see what the various major faiths have to say on the matter.

CHRISTIANITY

WAS ST. THOMAS AQUINAS SPEAKING FOR ALL OF CHRISTIANITY when he posited that touching yourself was worse than mating with your mother? Tough call.

BUDDHISM

MASTURBATION IS NOT A NO-NO FOR MOST BUDDHISTS, although some believe that sex distracts from the quest for enlightenment. They cite Buddha's First Sermon, in which he called the pursuit of sensual pleasure "vulgar, coarse, and ignoble." Sure, if you're doing it right.

HINDUISM

RATHER THAN CONDEMN MASTURBATION, THE KAMA SUTRA explains how best to do it: "Churn your instrument with a lion's pounce: sit with legs stretched out at right angles to one another, propping yourself up with two hands planted on the ground between them, and rub it between your arms." Few boys require coaching in this activity.

ISLAM

FOR MUSLIMS, MASTURBATION, KNOWN AS *TIMNA*, IS FORBIDDEN. Period.

HEFNERISM

FOR THE WORSHIPPERS OF HEDONISM, MOST ARTFULLY PRACTICED as it is preached by Sir Hugh of Hefner, masturbation is regarded as a natural way to relieve stress and provide yourself with pleasure. He even offers helpful pictures to get you started.

MY ADVICE

AGAIN, PRIVATE PARTS ARE PRIVATE. "IF YOU FEEL ITCHY AND THINK only rubbing yourself will make it feel better, do so alone in your room—but do as little as possible, or you could scrape and injure yourself. And, by the way, what makes you want to do that, and what do you think about?" Freaking out over your son's new hobby never works.

HOMOSEXUALITY: GAYETY IN THE LAITY

IT'S NOT A GOOD TIME IN HISTORY TO BE CLOSED-MINDED OR judgmental about a kid's decision to come out. In this (mostly) enlightened society, there are wonderful alternatives to freaking out—like love, compassion, tolerance, and even encouragement.

Many Christians condemn homosexuality, but a 1997 stance taken by U.S. Catholic bishops announced that while "morality presumes the freedom to choose…homosexual orientation is experienced as a given, not as something freely chosen. By itself, therefore, a homosexual orientation cannot be considered sinful."

The Church has enough trouble explaining the actions of its own offending priests, so I will not pontificate further except to say how sad it all is—and that it needs fixing.

As for the Jews, it was in Leviticus that Moses admonished, "You should not lie with man as with woman," but many take a view akin to that of the Catholic bishops: if homosexuality can be shown by science to be a natural state, then it must have been created by God and cannot be considered wrong.

There is controversy about whether Buddha allowed gays among his followers. The Dalai Lama caused a ruckus during a visit to San Francisco when he declared that gay and lesbian liaisons are "generally considered sexual misconduct."

A section of the Kama Sutra focuses on gay men, known as "the third sex." It also mentions women who have sex with other women (usually because they can't find men) and advises them on which garden vegetables can serve as useful instruments of satisfaction.

Most monks and nuns are celibate, but centuries ago, Tibetan monks actually made crude sex toys. I thought you'd want to know.

IS IT PREMARITAL SEX IF YOU DON'T PLAN TO GET MARRIED?

HINDUS POINT ADMIRINGLY TO GANDHI, WHO TOOK HIS VOW OF chastity and then had virgins sleep nude with him to "test his resolve." George Clooney tried this and failed miserably. "What Islam fears most in unregulated sexuality is its ability to cause social chaos," says one scholar. As a result, Muslim cultures often segregate men and women. Female genital mutilation shortly before puberty is also common in many countries, although the women who perform the operation sometimes can be persuaded to "leave some fire for the husband."

BAD BOYS IN OTTAWA

MY SONS MIGHT WANT TO BYPASS THIS STORY, UNTOLD thus far in any record of Thicke family history, appearing as it does near the top of my list of "Not My Most Celebrated Dad Moments."

I was twenty years old and a budding star at the Canadian Broadcasting Corporation, having just recorded the theme song to the *Miss Teen Canada Pageant*. A beauty pageant can be a watershed moment in a young man's life, if not the highlight of a musical career, and I capitalized by making friends with a particularly winsome runner-up from our capital city of Ottawa. She invited me to visit, and weeks later I did just that along with a buddy. (He's now married to a glamorous Hollywood star with a glamorous twenty-something daughter currently poised to become a glamorous star herself. I'd love to name names but... that would be unglamorous.)

So pumped was Miss Teen Ottawa's dad about the fact that his daughter knew a guy on TV that he threw a party celebrating our arrival that Friday night, to which he invited aunts, uncles, cousins, and his entire office staff. My pal and I were hits, telling jokes, playing guitars, and generally knocking the cover off the ball until the hour approached midnight and one particularly drunken legal secretary made a startling proposition: "Let's go somewhere and ****!" (Vernacular reference to adult activity, disguised in case your kids look over your shoulder.) Any male will understand the impact this sort of invitation has on a twenty-year-old libido, coming as it did from a buxom, highly available woman only a few years older but obviously with a vast experiential advantage. And yet I politely declined, a decision for which I expect to go to heaven.

But not so fast.

Apparently, I wasn't the only irresistible item on the menu that night, because minutes later my partner breathlessly dragged me into a corner—he was just a little drunker than the legal secretary—and bellowed, "Guess what!?" I guessed right, but he continued anyway. "That secretary just said, 'Let's go somewhere and ****,' and...and...she said you can come, too." This was becoming too bizarre to ignore, but I held my ground, sort of. I must have said something like, "We can't leave this party, but keep me posted," because I got the news bulletin fifteen minutes later that a motel room had been booked and the three of us were going to slip away on the premise that we'd be driving this vixen home. Soon I and the two drunks were in a Jimmy Swaggart-level roadside dive trying to figure out what to do next. From what I recall, anything would have been fine for the secretary, but my friend was tripping and falling a lot, so after more stumbling and some awkward grappling, the secretary fell asleep. This was actually a relief to us fellas, for whom the situation had quickly gone from "incredible opportunity" to "bad idea."

We drove Jezebel home and returned to our host's house, by which time the revelers were gone, the lights were off, and Brian—that's the co-scoundrel's name—tiptoed into our quarters while I gravitated to the kitchen light, still on, and a morose father sitting alone at the table with a cup of coffee, head bowed, jacket off, and tie loosened. "Hey," I articulated in a situation for which there were no words. After a moment he looked up and our eyes met. "We got your secretary home safely." A faint smile crept across his face, as if to acknowledge his own folly along with mine. "It's OK," he said. But it wasn't. To this day, it's not OK with me, and for months that followed, I wrote impassioned letters begging forgiveness without ever getting a response. I was simply not the kind of guy he'd want his daughter to see again—ever. Now that's a good dad. As for me, it's unfortunate that guilt turns out to be one of our most recurrent and profound teachers.

SEX BY THE NUMBERS

- Half of all high school students have had sex.
- Nearly half of all pregnancies are unintended, with 835,000 U.S. teenage pregnancies annually.
- Frequency of sex:

  18- to 29-year-olds: 112 times a year

  30- to 39-year-olds: 86 times a year

  40- to 49-year-olds: 69 times a year

(I don't have figures for those over fifty, but you can bet we're grateful for every one.)

- By age twenty-five, half of all Americans will get a sexually transmitted disease (STD).
- There are eight STDs. Can you name them?
- How fast do sperm swim? Seven miles per hour. Make sure your kids know they can't outrun the little suckers, either.
- More than 80 percent of women are monogamous in marriage, compared to 65 percent of men. That means 35 percent of the married men cheat in America. The rest cheat in Europe.

DEFINITION

GROUP SEX: WHEN YOU HAVE A PARTNER.

All kidding aside, it is possible that no area of your children's lives will offer more potential for happiness and misery. None will offer more choices, require more decisions, or lead to more consequences. Ahead are lifelong influences, life-altering pitfalls, and life-affirming heights.

Overall, your advice must include the four R's:

- Restraint
- Respect
- Responsibility
- Reproduction

Be sure to talk about pregnancy, disease, delight, and—the big sell here—love!

Carter had his first kiss in the third grade, on the cheek from an irresistible lass named Madison. Describing his good fortune that evening, he exclaimed, "I've gotta keep a file on this. I'll call it 'the greatest day of my life.'"

15 Faith

God Help Us!

SHOULD YOU LET THEM FIND THEIR OWN GOD? BE WARNED THAT it might be SpongeBob SquarePants. Better to guide them toward one you're familiar with, even though your own relationship with the deity may have been hit-and-miss and your place in the afterlife is not yet assured because of some technicality from your college days.

This chapter will be short, because you really must find your own way on this subject. What do you believe in so strongly, with such commitment, that you're prepared to bet the farm on this roll of the dice? That, when all else fails, is where you'll want your kids to turn to. What do you want them to know above all—to count on, trust, and have faith in? What universal truths about a Higher Court, Ultimate Power, and Infinite Being will guide them when you can't? Make sure you believe, then tell them how you did it, empowering them with a set of Almighty values that will kick in when they can't make sense of the world around them.

FIRST FAITH

RELIGION, AFTER ALL, BEGAN AS A MEANS OF CURBING FEAR BY controlling the multitudes, who were afraid when they saw lightning and fire and carnivores larger than themselves. In these early days of fast food (if you weren't fast, you were food), these primitive people needed a place to turn for assurance that things would be OK and that they wouldn't be devoured in the middle of the night. Without a lock on the cave or a gun under the bed, you'd get much better sleep if you believed that a supernatural power was on your side. Unfortunately, there was scant evidence that God was intervening on the safety front—no news of a Divine Hand smiting a saber-toothed tiger about to pounce on a screaming sprinter in a loincloth whose only defense was a pathetic pointy rock tethered to the end of a stick. That caveman didn't have a prayer, and apparently God was saving his best tricks for later on, when Charlton Heston was young.

The forward thinkers in these barefoot communities thought up extravagant rituals to get God's attention on the "Help!" front. If hordes of believers dancing around a campfire appeased the Almighty, surely burning one of your neighbors alive would make a big impression. An offering of human entrails for God to nibble on would no doubt be remembered fondly at some critical moment, and some children tied to a stake on a mountain where God could see them would seal the deal altogether. Fear and hysteria were important elements in starting any new religion. Let us pray.

HOME

HOME IS WHERE IT STARTS. READ BIBLE STORIES AT BEDTIME, a little Moses and Noah mixed in with their *Green Eggs and Ham*. The ritual of bowing heads at dinner and giving thanks for blessings, such as family and health and potatoes and lamb chops, reminds us of our good fortune, the importance of treasuring those wondrous things, and the comforting thought that some omnipotent benevolence has got our back and will reward us for righteous living. The value of prayer will become most evident when your child is afraid of thunder, when the turtle dies, or when she disappears on a Spring Break road trip with a guy named Woody who has $40 and sixty tattoos.

CHURCH

IT'S NOT IMPORTANT THAT YOUR CHILDREN ATTEND CHURCH for any particular reason. There is no "right" reason for worship. My own church activity as a youth had questionable motivations: I joined the Catholic Youth Group because they had the best hockey team, while I simultaneously enrolled in the Protestant Club because they had the better picnics. By doing so I was bi-denominational and bi-seasonal, by far the most uncommitted—but curious—ecclesiast in the village.

However, I was still in a church environment, and that was a good thing. Kids will resist because they won't want to get up early on Sunday and they'll hate wearing fancy shoes on the weekend, but if you can get them in the tent, religious training will have a chance. It is important that your children have an awareness of every religion, because in our homogeneous global society, we're seeing the removal of racial, ethnic, and religious barriers, a trend that I hope will one day lead us to become one gigantic family. (I'm not holding my breath on that one. I don't even like everybody in my current family.) Carter learned about Kwanzaa in the first grade, and I will encourage him to learn about Buddhism, Hinduism, and Islam—beyond the superficial, and often inflammatory, portrayals we get on the six o'clock news.

GOOD OMENS FROM ABOVE

- 86 percent of teenagers pray.
- 91 percent believe their prayers are answered.
- 77 percent pray for a sick friend or relative.
- 72 percent pray for personal needs.
- 51 percent pray for world peace or other global preservation.
- 23 percent pray for material things.

DEFEND YOUR FAITH

IF YOU TEACH THEM THAT GOD WATCHES EVERYTHING, CARES for them, and has all the answers, be prepared to answer questions about evil and suffering, disease, earthquakes, and Osama. Get ready to explain death, and don't make heaven sound so good that you diminish the value of life. "Does a spirit leave your body? Will Snuggles the Cat see Aunt Martha the Wheezer up there?" Rent *The Lion King* again.

Faith can take center stage in teaching morality, and the old, reliable "fear of God" can assist with the discipline part. Early behavior is instantaneous, reflexive reaction, whereas later elective behavior results from thought, choice, value judgments, and a consideration of the consequences. "Right and wrong" become differentiated when wrong gets an asswhuppin'.

"What would God think?" is a notion that occurs only in families that believe in God, but I do not presume to put that pressure on you. Agnostics buy books and raise kids, too.

AGNOSTICS/ATHEISTS

WHAT IS AN AGNOSTIC? SOMEBODY WHO DOESN'T BELIEVE in Gnostics? And what does an atheist believe in? Maybe it's just the conviction that there is no God; in that case, why bother praying and learning all those dreary songs, if the only thing we really have faith in is that we are on our own and have to trust ourselves and each other? If that's what you believe, I wish you the best of luck, because I certainly don't trust myself, and I'm not really sure about you either. For those of us always on the lookout for tangible evidence of God's existence, we nevertheless hope, despite the lack of direct scientific proof, that there is indeed a Greater Hand watching over us. Sharing that belief with family and friends is one of life's great bonding possibilities.

CHICK MAGNET

AT THE AGE OF FOUR, CARTER CAME UP WITH THE MOST CREATIVE and flattering compliment imaginable. Tanya had been primping and dressing before she finally emerged from the closet in full-bloom Charity Fundraiser Banquet Formal Finery. Carter gave her the once-over and declared, "Wow, Tanya! You are pretty enough to be God's girlfriend!" She was on cloud nine all night, and anything I might have said would have paled in comparison. Thanks Carter, for a great evening.

AFFLUENZA

MANY CHILDREN, AS WELL AS ADULTS, SUFFER FROM THE SPIRITUAL poverty of believing that things, rather than character and service, are what matter in life. Affluenza is contagious—kids can catch it from parents and friends.

CONCLUSION

IF NOT STRUCTURED RELIGION, AT LEAST MAKE SURE YOUR CHILD grows up with the "do unto others" values and principles shared by most faiths.

THE PROVERBIAL LAUGH

HERE'S SOMETHING I FOUND FOR YOU ON THE INTERNET. I didn't get these from a Christian joke site, but there probably is such a place. Look it up if you dare.

A first-grade teacher collected some proverbs, gave each kid in class the first half of each proverb, and asked them to fill in the rest.

- Don't bite the hand that…looks dirty.
- You can't teach an old dog…math.
- If you lie down with dogs, you…will stink in the morning.
- An idle mind is…the best way to relax.
- A penny saved is…not much.
- Two is company, three's…the Musketeers.
- Children should be seen and not…spanked or grounded.
- If at first you don't succeed…get new batteries.
- When the blind lead the blind…get out of the way.
- There is no fool like…Aunt Edith.

The kids also came up with their own proverbial wisdom to share with one another:

- When your dad is mad and asks, "Do I look stupid?" don't answer.
- Never tell your mom her diet's not working.
- Puppies still have bad breath, even after eating a Tic Tac.
- If you want a kitten, start out by asking for a horse.

16 Happiness

When Money, Sports, Sex, and God Aren't Enough

KNOWING THAT ONE OF OUR BIG JOBS IS TO IMPART VALUES, here are some well-accepted platitudes:

- The secret of happiness is to count your blessings while others are adding up their troubles.
- Happiness is the feeling you're feeling when you want to keep feeling it.
- For every minute you're angry, you lose sixty seconds of happiness.
- You'll be happier if you'll give people a bit of your heart rather than a piece of your mind.

"HOW FAMILIES ARE FARING," AN ARTICLE BY GINI KOPECKY WALLACE (FAMILY CIRCLE)

THIS SURVEY INDICATED THAT THE HAPPIEST FAMILY TYPE WAS "Married, No Kids," with an "excellent" report of 40 percent on the "Ain't Life Grand" meter. Presumably, these self-absorbed sods just don't know what they're missing. Anyway, they don't read books like these, so I'm safe to speculate. "Married, Young Kids at Home" had a 25 percent "Lucky Us" factor, which was, remarkably enough, the same score reported for "Single, Young Kids at Home." The "Single, Grown Kids Elsewhere" group was miserable, with a 15 percent "I've Got Nobody" rating.

More adults in the happiest group know all their neighbors, are satisfied with the number of friends they have, and feel good about the number of relatives living nearby to whom they can turn in an emergency. High-HQ (happiness quotient) people are also more likely to belong to a church, mosque, or synagogue and attend services weekly. More are registered politically and vote regularly, and more parents in the top group have saved enough to pay for their children's education, their own retirement, and whatever setbacks the future may hold.

THE HUMOR GENE

WHAT ACTIVITY RELAXES MUSCLES, REDUCES BLOOD PRESSURE, exercises the abdomen, boosts the immune system, and releases pain-fighting hormones?

The answer is laughter. Thank you, Will Ferrell, Seth Rogen, Kathy Griffin, Chris Rock, Wanda Sykes, Lewis Black, Jamie Foxx, Kat Williams, George Lopez, Tosh.O, and Chelsea Handler.

Muscle tension remains low for up to forty-five minutes after a session of vigorous laughter, and a real belly laugh can relax the muscles more than a vigorous massage. And those are just the physical benefits. Laughter can also provide emotional distance from distressing situations by finding the humor where others see only the aggravation. Attitude is often the difference between tragedy and comedy, so be sure to pass a good one on to your children.

HUMOR DEFICIENCY SYNDROME

DO YOU LIGHT UP A ROOM JUST BY LEAVING IT? DOES YOUR dinner conversation revolve around your backache, sore feet, food allergies, and cholesterol readings? When someone tells you a joke, do you groan and point out that it's politically incorrect or not funny? It is not necessary to constantly denigrate yourself with false modesty, but self-deprecating humor shows that you're human and that you're confident enough to poke fun at the dweeb in the mirror. Keeping your own humor collection will ensure that you have comic relief when you need it most. A diary of your baby's most amusing moments will do nicely.

BUBBLES IN THE BATHTUB

THERE ARE A HUNDRED WAYS TO MAKE KIDS LAUGH THAT involve bodily functions. There's no end to the jokes and pranks, rhymes and dances, tricks and games guaranteed to delight children, but the old reliable Bathroom Humor never misses, spanning the progression from infant to toddler to grade schooler to adolescence, when this hilarity becomes an art form.

RONNIE DASH—LAST BAD DAD CONFESSION

YES, I ALWAYS PREFACE CARTER'S FAVORITE STORY BY REMINDING him that it's another good example of a bad example from the "Don't Do

What I Do, Do What I Say" collection. This was also my mother's favorite story to tell, so apparently some trace of mean-spirited, perverse humor runs in the family. The occasion was my sixth birthday party. With only one first-grade class in our small-town school, everybody knew everybody else, and you couldn't have a birthday party without inviting the entire group.

In every classroom, however, there will be at least one person who isn't your child's friend, one person your perfect, precious son will not get along with—for reasons obviously attributable to that nasty other kid. For me, that first-grade nemesis was Ronnie Dash. He was Sammy Hagar to my David Lee Roth, Liza Minelli to that lizard she married for a minute and a half, Glenn Beck to, well, everybody. When it came time to pass out the invitations, I protested to my mother, but she correctly pointed out that a birthday party would be a pleasant, festive environment in which I might start a new relationship with Ronnie. This seemed like a long shot, since I usually wanted to strangle the little troll, and I'm sure he felt the same about me.

I later learned that his mother, Sophie, had called my mother to remind her that being left out could be damaging to Ronnie's psyche. Not only that, but "a birthday party would be a pleasant, festive environment in which to start a new relationship." Moms think alike that way.

On the day of the party, Ronnie showed up looking great—hair slicked back, even a bowtie. I welcomed him at the door and was careful to take immediate possession of the gift he brought before locking him in the backyard. "Let me in," he begged, as he scurried from window to window in the snow. "No," I carpe diemed. My mother heard Ronnie's cries for help and rescued him from hypothermia, and although the rest of the party went smoothly enough, Ronnie held enough of a grudge that he told his mother, who made a follow-up call the next day. I'm not sure exactly what was said, but the conversation ended with a threat by

Mrs. Dash to kick the stuffing out of my mom. Mrs. Dash was a large woman, and I suspect she was perfectly capable of doing just that. After the Dash clash, I never harassed Ronnie again, but Carter loves to relive the tale over and over. Some legends never die.

THE [YOUR NAME HERE] SITCOM

MY REAL-LIFE FAMILY WOULD HAVE MADE A GOOD SITCOM. They made me laugh, anyway. I'll bet you've often thought the same about yours. Maybe our families together would be a hit sitcom. Have your people call my people and we'll do lunch.

* * *

When Brennan was six, I took him to the ballet. Attentive as always, he noticed how all the girls danced on their tiptoes. Afterwards I asked, "How'd you like it?"

He said, "Fine, but why don't they just get taller girls?"

* * *

When Robin was five, he saw a TV commercial for a laxative and asked, "What does irregularity mean?" I replied that it means you can't go number two, to which he said, "Why don't they just go number one twice?"

* * *

As we sat in a restaurant waiting for a friend, Carter, at age three, watched a 300-pound man come in and observed, quite rightly, "That man's fat."

I said, "He's coming over to sit with us and you'll hurt his feelings if you say he's fat, so don't say he's fat."

The guy came over and sat down, and I made the introductions. "Carter, this is my friend, Darryl."

Carter said, "Hi, Darryl. You're not fat."

We chatted, Darryl left, and Carter spotted another fellow, this one with gigantic ears, each one the size of a car door. Carter said, "That man has funny ears."

I say, "He's also a friend of mine, so if he comes over, don't say he's got funny ears." Carter asks, "Can I say 'Big Ears'?"

"No, don't say 'Big Ears' either."

Sure enough, Dumbo strolled over and I said, "Carter, this is John."

"Hi, John," Carter said. "What kind of ears are those?"

* * *

When Carter turned four, I exclaimed, "Hey, big boy, you're not three anymore."

He said, "Oh. Am I still Carter?"

* * *

Laughter sometimes comes from our anxieties about a changing world. On Carter's fourth Christmas, while he was trimming the tree, he picked up the three wise men, noticed the camels and turbans, and whispered, "Psst...Dad...Taliban."

I laughed, but it was one of those nervous "loss of innocence" reactions. Expect those.

MOM JOKES

MOM WAS TERRIFIC IN EVERY WAY EXCEPT FOR COOKING. She didn't have much confidence, so she would overcook. My mother would burn, she'd cremate, she'd nuke. Put it this way: if you are what you eat, I'd be black.

- Mom's idea of a balanced meal was one that gave you a 50–50 chance of survival.
- We had to learn the Heimlich maneuver for when her coffee got stuck in Dad's throat.
- Her TV dinners gave us the reruns.
- After a while, we gave up on the TV dinners and started sucking them frozen. Ever had a broccoli popsicle?
- We'd throw the dog table scraps and he'd throw them back.
- I was in college before I learned that toast didn't have bones.
- We finally bought her a microwave so she could screw things up faster.

(Those were the jokes, folks. Truth be told, Mom was the best.)

Second Families

"If You're So Cool, Why is Mom Living with Her Trainer?"

ONE THING A COOL PARENT NEVER LIKES TO CONSIDER IS THAT the day could come when he or she is a divorced cool parent. If you are ever this unfortunate—breaking up a family is never pretty—it's then that the cool part must come into play, as in "keeping your cool" and the famous "cooling-off period."

HOW DO YOU KNOW WHEN IT'S REALLY OVER?

DIVORCE IS A GOOD CLUE. BARRING THAT, IF SHE DRAWS A chalk line around your body every time you lie down, odds are she's not happy.

THE D-WORD

HAVE YOU DONE ALL YOU CAN TO SAVE THE MARRIAGE? This is your child's only chance at the ideal family unit, and his life will never be the same afterwards, so be very sure before you pull the plug and consign him to a lifetime of divided loyalties and split schedules.

THE CHILD'S BEST INTERESTS

YOU MAY HAVE ALREADY BLOWN THAT, SINCE DIVORCE IS SELDOM in the child's best interests, no matter how much rationalizing you do to justify your filing. The first thing disillusioned and dissolutioning adults promise themselves is that the kids will always come first, and that's about as easy to do as obeying all Ten Commandments for one calendar year. Public civility is important, but the best-intentioned, most enlightened couples have trouble faking affection for each other once they have made that fateful decision. Insults feel good but accomplish little, so you may want to save your best for e-mail:

"You put the 'ho' in 'home,' baby."

"Really? Well you are in the meaning of 'pollutant,' the residue caught in the filter of my life."

"Oh yeah? May you get hit by a bus as you walk through the streets of hell, sweetheart."

"You need to find yourself? Try looking in the dictionary under 'selfish, cheating bastard.'"

AND SO IT GOES

E-MAIL MAY BE THE BEST MEANS OF COMMUNICATION BETWEEN you and your ex from now on, because you'll have a never-ending list of parental decisions to make together involving custody (50-50 or weekends?), holidays (not fair if one gets Christmas and the other gets Martha Stewart's birthday), and school. My ex wanted to spend $15K on a private school in California so our first-grader could learn Spanish. I pointed out that at public schools, the kids were already speaking it for free. He's in a private school. Even religious upbringing can become an issue, if, for instance, your kid started out Catholic and your ex marries a rabbi.

These kinds of disagreements are how parents go nuts and attorneys buy vacation homes, so agree on as many terms as possible before involving the lawyers.

MINE'S BIGGER THAN YOURS

THERE IS NO AVOIDING THE SUBCONSCIOUS UNDERCURRENT OF competition, because whether it's more toys, more trips to the zoo, or more hours of TV or stories per night, you will want to be your son's confidant or your daughter's best friend, not second best. The competition cycle could cause you to try harder, spend more, make bad judgments, and ultimately ruin your most important creation. It is often difficult to be a stern disciplinarian because of the ever-present fear that your former spouse is saying "yes" all the time while you're saying "no." Sorry, but at times it's more important to be right than popular.

EXPLAINING WHAT WENT WRONG

YOU THOUGHT IRAQ AND KATRINA WERE CONTROVERSIAL! SEE IF you and your ex can at least concur as to why you split up so that, when he's old enough to hear it, your child can live his life with a single interpretation, one story to tell when people ask—which they will. As always, conversations must be age appropriate and evenhanded, minimally judgmental, and painted over with a happy face wherever possible.

"DUDE, HOW'D YOU BLOW IT?"

TO ENSURE THAT HISTORY DOESN'T REPEAT ITSELF, TRY to understand what it is about you that people hate—or at least what didn't work for your mate. Did you book the wrong restaurants? Play too much golf? Bring home lousy friends? Did you cheat? Suffocate? Intimidate? Underestimate?

Give yourself the fitness test. Are you qualified? Are you healed? Rehabilitated? Wiser? Better? Is there a "new and improved" version ready for recycling? Get a reliable emotional mirror and take a cold, hard look to see who you are, determining not only what you need but what you have to offer this time around. Get opinions and "reviews" from friends, maybe even your children. How much time, energy, and capital will you have left after attending to existing responsibilities, such as career, your softball team, your mother, and your kids? Do you value alone time? Remember that marriage changes things. (You'll probably find yourself dating less.)

Most "previously owned" adults fall into three categories:

1. Those willing to find another relationship.
2. Those who'd rather be widowed or gay.
3. Those who'd rather get poked in the eye with a hot stick hourly.

If a second marriage is in the cards, the child is about to have a new family. If you and your ex both remarry, suddenly the kid has three families to deal with—the original and two offshoots—not to mention the multiple sets of step-grandparents, semi-uncles, pseudo-aunts, and quasi-cousins. The potential for confusion is staggering when Christmas can only be arranged by an air traffic controller.

Congratulations if you have recovered and feel strong and secure enough to plunge ahead, undaunted, unafraid of a second try. Or a third. People on their fourth should be daunted.

THE DREAM VERSION

WHO WANTS TO MARRY MY DAD? THAT TV GEM GOT IT RIGHT ABOUT one thing: the next choice must be done by committee. The casual dating experiments do not have to be detailed to the kids, and one-night stands at your house with strangers from the gym are a no-no. The first time he or she visits could possibly be explained away as an act of charity for a homeless strumpet, but you'll need answers when a relationship gets more serious.

He or she must fit in with your child, which is not to say that the kid gets to pick: the qualities we seek in a mate are not necessarily the same ones he admires. Find a way to make the child feel he's in the loop by at least informing him at regular steps along the way about what could become a new household arrangement.

In many cases the child will resist, not wanting to share you or your house or, worse yet, not liking the proposed new cohabitant. ("OK, this has been fun, now when is she leaving?") Monitor your child's reactions to these news bulletins. Throwing up when she enters the room or lurking around your gun collection are sure signs that it's not going well.

If you're freshly on the market, there's a chance you have a teenager who's also single and looking. This is one of life's perversely curious coincidences that you'll just have to deal with—offering advice and establishing boundaries without being a total, transparent hypocrite.

THE WISH LIST

RESPECT YOUR KIDS' FEELINGS ABOUT THE ADULT COMPANY you seek, but hold firm to your personal, well-earned Dos and Don'ts list for finding Mr. or Ms. Righter Than The Last One. Here's mine.

- Where to look. Remember where and how you met the ex—then look elsewhere. The new mate will want to stake out her own territory, and both of you will be better off with fewer "been there, done thats." Dating services specialize in finding compatible partners, and judging by your last choice, you need help.
- Compatibility. If she likes to jog at 6 a.m. and your first cigarette is scheduled for 7:30 a.m., your soulmate search may not be finished.
- Kid Rock or Bach? Try to start with things in common, such as music, or you'll hate what gets programmed on the car radio, not to mention the person in the passenger seat.
- Sex—every day or once a month? Remember that problem from the first marriage?
- The package deal. Assuming no one's perfect, go for overall compatibility. It's like this, ma'am: If he scores a 6 in household repairs, 7 in money management, 8 in bed, and 9 in family values, that's 30 out of a possible 40 points—a better bet than three 10s and a 0 in family values. And what will you change to score higher on his list?

DATING DO-OVERS

DATING IS A COMPLICATED SCIENCE, AND THERE ARE FEW PLACES to look for reliable advice. If your kid chooses you as a source, maybe you can teach him so he doesn't make your mistakes. I've had some lousy dates, and I've learned the following things from them:

o Get references. These can include phone numbers of the last hearts she ripped out and stomped on, guys who found her impossible to live with and were tired of putting up with her crap. And what will she learn about you if she does the same?

o Never faint at a Halloween party at the Playboy Mansion. I did, and it tends to embarrass your date and make you look wimpy. It's a long story (not that I've shown any reluctance to tell those so far), so suffice it to say it involved a long plane ride, sleep deprivation, dehydration, stress—the standard excuses—and that I passed out in the middle of the circular driveway in front of a crowd of people who were waiting for their vehicles and had no time for a dead man. Young punk sitcom actors were stepping over my horizontal body and pointing down in recognition. "Hey! That's Dr. Seaver!" before stepping over me and walking away to make small talk with the body-painted party favors. I was the centerpiece among centerfolds. To make it more bizarre, this was costume night—I was a hockey player and my date was Jessica Rabbit—which made for a colorful couple at the hospital. Yes, hospital. The ambulance arrived, and I was soon hooked up to an IV, an ignominious first for Playboy guests. The message: many women prefer "strong and competent" to "prone and lifeless."

SIGNIFICANT OTHER?

THERE'S A ROMANTIC TERM. THIS WAS A PHRASE COINED BY THE same guy who came up with "Bloody Show" for that childbirth spectacle. Significant Other? How about Incredible Relief, Viable Alternative, Palpable Paramour, or Substantial and Recurrent Codependent Elective? "Honey" or "Sugar" may still work, depending on which side of the Mason-Dixon Line you grew up on.

PHOTOPHOBIA

"WHO'S THAT WOMAN ON YOUR LAP, DAD?" HOW MANY TIMES did Gary Hart hear that?

One of the challenges in second families will be the question of what to do with memorabilia from the first family. When a new mate enters the picture, he or she won't be comfortable with a lot of photos around the house or in scrapbooks that include your ex. Keep in mind, however, that the child may be comforted by the missing mother or father's presence, even if only in a token photograph—consider placing them in the child's bedroom.

For the living room, I know it's tough to part with that shot of you and the ex with Barry Bonds or Jessica Biel, but who said relationships didn't require sacrifice?

Tanya drew the line at the wedding albums of the two previous bosses. My argument was that those collections included family members, some deceased, whom I wanted to remember as they were in those days. The broader "child's best interests" argument is that kids deserve to see what their birth parents looked like in happier times that somehow explain their own origins.

SECOND WEDDING PROTOCOL

DISTRIBUTE RESPONSIBILITIES FAIRLY. YOU MAY HAVE MULTIPLE candidates for ring boy, flower girl, maid of honor, best man, etc., but God forbid the daughter from the first marriage has a bigger assignment than the son from the second marriage when she officiates at the third marriage.

WILL YOU HAVE MORE KIDS?

IF I DO IT AGAIN, WATCH FOR ME TO BE ONE OF THOSE HOARY old actors with a baby at sixty and a teenager at seventy-five. I don't want to be teaching my son to drive just when they're revoking my license. I don't want my wife changing two sets of diapers if one of them is mine. Nevertheless, if your kids are what you've lived for, the delight of your life, these are the kinds of choices you make.

I'll keep you posted on the website.

WHY YOUNGER WOMEN?

THE AGE FACTOR WILL BE ONE CONSIDERATION WHEN MAKING choices appropriate to your child's sensibilities. "Dating" is a creepy concept for a middle-aged man, since most of the women available for communing are younger than me, but so are some countries, like Namibia and Belarus. One girl told her mother she was dating me, and her mother said I should be carbon-dated. I don't want to be on the Seniors Dating Tour, and I hate being in clubs where I feel like the chaperone. The last dance I learned was the twist.

What is the appeal of younger women? (A reminder that "younger" is a relative term. If you're fifty, you're younger and I love you for it!) In fact, the so-called "cougar" demographic is ideal...the package: looks, smarts, independence. The questions arise in the May-December age spread. Such as...

a) "What do you talk about?" "Me."
b) Young women don't know any better, because they haven't been jerked around, disappointed, and embittered by guys like us. Sorry, I don't presume to speak for you, but most haven't seen our B.S. before and probably can't even imagine some of it.
c) With any luck, it will take them longer to spot our faults—we have decades of experience trying to cover up our inadequacies—and that edge in years buys us time to work on the stuff they'll hate.
d) Younger women don't have baggage. And I don't mean kids—I would never call my sons baggage. Mortgages and someone else's health plans are baggage. And you might have an ex who's a regular Samsonite outlet. And speaking of bags...
e) If I wanted to feel a saggy ass, I'd grab my own. The May-December thing may seem superficial, but some of us can be shallow on many levels, not just looks.

f) Young girls don't have lawyers yet!

On a less facetious note, an unfair trend of age-ism still exists in romance. We teach our kids to be open-minded, so we profess to be blind to racial, religious, financial, and ancestral disparities in encouraging couples to couple. Why not drop the age-gap prejudice, too, if it works for the two incurable romantics involved?

HUMOR, NOW MORE THAN EVER

IF MARRIAGE REQUIRES A SENSE OF HUMOR TO ENJOY, SURELY divorce requires a sense of humor to survive.

"My ex was a great housekeeper. We had two houses—she kept both of them."

– Martin Mull

OTHER WORDS OF WISDOM

- Marriage is when a man finds out what kind of fellow his wife would have preferred.
- Marriage is like golf—it looks easy but takes a lot of balls.
- Marriage is the number one cause of divorce.
- Half of all marriages end in divorce. The rest end in death.
- Marriage? If you want something that lasts a lifetime, get herpes.
- You want magic? Date Siegfried and Roy. (I hope he's feeling better.)
- "My ex said I was not her type. I considered that a compliment."
- "She thought it a plus that she was honest and didn't hold things in. Personally, I wish she would have."
- "Happily married" may be an oxymoron for cynics, but it's one of life's worthy goals, right up there with tighter abs and a clean prostate exam.

My parents were married forty-three years. I'd like to do that, too—at least cumulatively.

FACTOID

Anyone who tells you they're not a good person probably knows what they're talking about.

18 Legacy

They're Finally Legal!

THE BIG "EIGHTEEN" SEEMS LIKE A MAGIC NUMBER IN TERMS of passing the torch to your kids—grown-ups at last—but the truth is, we never stop parenting. In fact, the stakes are higher now than ever. Will they have success? Will they find love? Live long and healthy lives? Will they give you grandchildren and put another generation at risk?

WHAT WILL YOUR KIDS REMEMBER ABOUT YOU?

CHILDHOOD ALZHEIMER'S WILL AFFECT YOUR FAMILY, TOO. I'm not being disrespectful—my grandfather had Alzheimer's—but your son will have no memory of you taking him to Disney World when he was two. It will sadden you that he doesn't remember Grandma, who died when he was three. He'd have only vague memories of you if you left this world when he was five.

But your time together is what's important: he was falling in love with you while you were doing those things he can't remember. Your home video collection will stimulate their memories, and the stories you tell of those pictures will become family lore, a tribute to the ancestors as well as a sense of comfort and belonging for your child.

HOW TO THROW A BIRTHDAY PARTY FOR A ONE-YEAR-OLD

NO PRESSURE, BUT YOU'LL BE SETTING THE TONE FOR LIFE ON how to celebrate those special occasions that become the "emotional comfort foods" of your child's existence. Don't set any crazy precedents you can't top. Don't compete with the mom who booked Ronald McDonald, the Anaheim Ducks, and two of the actual Wiggles.

The following is partially plagiarized, but I don't know from where. It doesn't seem like world-beater intellectual property, so I'll pass it on, regrettably uncredited.

- Invite six children, maximum, to the one-year-old's party.
- Include at least one other parent or babysitter for every two kids.
- Make it clear when the party starts and ends. One hour is ample.
- Ask the parents to bring their child's own bottle and cups.
- Frosted cupcakes are fun but messy, which make them good for photos but lousy for clean-up. Your call.
- Throw any old covering on the table. At this age, fancy tablecloths and matching napkins will go unnoticed. Paper is fine as long as the kids aren't smoking.
- Have someone other than you take photos. (This is a good job for a grandparent and keeps them away from the liquor.)
- Let the children play. Don't try to organize games and don't whoop things up. Stay calm and don't be surprised if some children cry for no reason whatsoever.

Don't forget to:

- Put a candle on the birthday child's cupcake.
- Light it.
- Blow it out.
- Sing "Happy Birthday."
- When the party is over, give each little person a new rattle or toy as a party favor.
- Send everyone home.
- Have a drink and a bath.

THE GNARLY AUNT FIASCO

DON'T START TOO MANY HORRIBLE FAMILY TRADITIONS IF you want your children to look forward to calendar events every year. Hugging one aunt every Thanksgiving is enough for most kids. If there is a gaggle of aunts at one gathering, have the kids draw names from one of the aunts' ugly hats to see which aunt they'll kiss. How 'bout making one of the kids the Designated Aunt Kisser?

A SHANIA TWAIN CHRISTMAS

I REMEMBER THE EXCITEMENT AND ANTICIPATION OF THE ten-hour, dead-of-night car ride through the snow from Ottawa to Kirkland Lake every December with my parents. I had my favorite blanket and the back seat of the car all to myself as we passed the familiar landmarks: North Bay was the last "big city"—population 50,000—and that meant we had 150 miles to go. With no radio reception, the only sound was the rhythm of those squeaky windshield wipers slapping away the giant snowflakes, until the town of Englehart told us we were only thirty miles from home. (Shania will understand this—it's her neighborhood, and we like to publicize that. "Neighborhood," by the way, would be spelled "neighbourhood" in her neighborhood.)

Finally, by 3 a.m., the village of Kirkland Lake would become visible through the dark and silent night, and as we turned the corner down Tower Street, my heart skipped the proverbial beat when I saw the only lamp still glowing on the street, shining like a lighthouse from Is and Will's den. At least one of them was always standing guard, and when the silhouette appeared in the window, I knew it would be a grand Christmas, the kind you roll over in your mind for a lifetime, the kind of memories that make you who you are. Familiarity and repetition are important, and we must do whatever we can, whenever we can, to provide those moments year after year for our children.

ONE-ON-ONE IN THAILAND

NOTWITHSTANDING THE DACHAU DEBACLE, I GIVE ONE-ON-ONE vacations the highest recommendations. Depending on your household headcount, you'll have plenty of holidays as two parents and two kids, two parents and one kid, one parent and two kids—but I'm talking about one parent, one child, going someplace where every minute is spent together and every decision is made as a team.

What to have for breakfast, where to go, what to wear, what to do—it's all according to the buddy system. When Robin turned ten, I determined it would be a good time to take him on a birds-and-bees discussion trip, someplace where we could talk man to man. Now, ten is young, but in L.A., a guy could be married twice by then, in and out of rehab, and a millionaire from some stupid series. The other reason I decided on a one-on-one was that his thirteen-year-old brother simply had better things to do, and I was not in a grown-up relationship at the time, so no one else wanted to go with me.

Among the things you will learn about how your child's mind works 24/7 is just how much he knows about things you wish he didn't.

Strolling down a street in Bangkok, it is impossible to avoid those super-friendly fellows who offer to help tourists make new friends by arranging blind dates with super-friendly young women who are apparently available on a moment's notice, happy to display the more exotic attractions for which Thailand has become famous. The expression, "Want to meet student girl?" was repeated by many such entrepreneurs with no qualms about pitching such tutorials even in the presence of my ten-year-old. I got the impression there would have been student girls for both of us if we had expressed any interest. Robin seemed strangely aware of the proposition—curse MTV!—though I quickly explained to Mr. Matchmaker that doing homework with a tutor on this vacation would not be necessary, and that the student girls would have to find another study partner.

THE DEAD MEXICAN SOCIETY

I WANT TEARS WHEN I GO. NOW MARRIED TO A LATINA, HOWEVER, I have learned about some interesting customs that could make that problematic.

For many Mexicans, the end of October means it's time to prepare for Dia de los Muertos or "Day of the Dead" celebrations. Mexicans have some unique and wonderful traditions, the breakfast burrito being my personal favorite, but I have yet to keep my schedule open for a parade in chicken suits to honor loved ones who have died. Not that I don't miss my dearly departed, but I honor them with a remembrance on their birthday and again on the anniversary of their death. Mexicans are very efficient by lumping them all together on one occasion, but this somehow places my mother on the same level as Uncle Perv, and that doesn't seem fair, since her passing was a much tougher adjustment for me. Day of the Dead is not a sad occasion, however, although you would expect some Mexican PR firm to come up with a peppier title if they're trying to sell Death Day as a commercial concept. When is Heart Attack Day, and how do I get to the Rigor Mortis Festival?

Nevertheless, there is much rejoicing and feasting and merrymaking. Come to think of it, we did have a similar celebration when Uncle Perv passed. Maybe I'm part Mexican. Houses are decorated and streets are filled with bright orange marigolds and paper cutouts, open coffins, candied skulls for sale, and huge skeleton puppets dancing in procession. For children this could also be called the Day of Having Nightmares Forever. After the procession, family members take food and drink to the cemetery, where they light candles and spruce up the gravesites. I guess it's better to see people free from grief and smiling again, but personally I hope my loved ones simply become hysterical at my demise.

STAND UP!

IT'S IMPORTANT THAT YOUR CHILDREN STAND FOR SOMETHING, which is why it's important that you stand for something, whether political, sociological, or spiritual.

Do you support abortion, capital punishment, affirmative action, same-sex marriages, cheaper drug prices, endowments for the arts, and America's obligation to be the moral compass of the planet? Do you stand for a person's right to wear furs or a beaver's right to keep his butt where it belongs? Do you stand for profiling at the airports or the "everybody gets wanded and removes their stinky shoes" approach? Are you with the NRA or against them?

Personally, my hat's in the ring with environmental concerns like the Waterkeeper's Alliance, stem cell research, the oft-mentioned Dump Diabetes movement, as well as anything that has to do with children's health. Apropos of what you're reading, half of you should contact the National Fatherhood Initiative to receive their advice and commit your involvement, by e-mailing info@fatherhood.org.

PUT YOUR MONEY WHERE YOUR MOUTH IS

IF YOU JOIN PETA, BE AN ACTIVE ACTIVIST. FORM A VOLUNTEER fire squad to help the fire department save animals who have been driven from their habitat when fires ravage our forests every summer. Et cetera ad infinitum.

THE WORLD WE LEAVE THEM

IT'S IMPOSSIBLE TO IMAGINE THE WONDERS OF TECHNOLOGY and medicine that will change our children's world by the end of their century. For openers, their tenure will be closer to 100 than the seventy-odd years we can expect. My grandfather's world could never have imagined cell phones, e-mail, hip replacements, Viagra, *Borat/Brüno*, or that guy who got pregnant twice. Let's hope they get their personal flying machines, male birth control pills, and a yummy drink that cures cancer.

HOW CAN LOVE BE REAL IF YOU HAVE AN ARTIFICIAL HEART?

TECHNO-ORGANS SUCH AS THE BIO-ARTIFICIAL KIDNEY ARE A combination of living and manufactured parts, a cartridge full of tiny plastic fibers bearing thousands of working kidney cells. A bio-artificial liver is also in the works, along with heart, lung, and pancreas. Soon we will all be able to play God and not have to leave that responsibility entirely to Oprah and Dick Cheney. Scientists are screening human embryos for a wide range of congenital conditions, and future generations will be able to screen for intellect, hair color, eye color, etc. Therapeutic cloning could yield versatile stem cells to replace diseased ones.

What advances would you like your children to see, and what are you doing to make them happen?

WORDS FROM MY DAD, DR. BRIAN CHRISTOPHER THICKE

I NEVER REALLY TRIED TO BE ANYTHING BUT DAD AND NEVER ASKED THEM to be anything but kids.

I spent time with my kids, and I explained why we did things a certain way and had to behave a certain way. I never sent my kids anywhere that I couldn't take them, such as music lessons or hockey practice. And I always praised them when they did well or even not so well.

I tried to let them see the benefit and respect you get for good manners—be polite, shake people's hands—my kids always did these things, and people liked them for it. Being a doctor brought me respect, but I reminded them that it was because doctors have good ethics and strong morals.

They knew I trusted them and that, since I had integrity, I expected them to have integrity, too. I always told them, "If you tell the truth, you never have to remember what you said."

Excuses were not accepted, but if they explained to me why something happened, then it was OK. Alan's line, "I didn't ask to be a kid," never really worked with me.

They also knew that while it was beneficial to come from a good background, you can't be successful without setting goals and working hard. In our house, it was a given that everyone went to university.

MY LEGACY ACCORDING TO BRENNAN

YOU WERE THERE WHEN I WAS BORN. YOU LET ME GROW WITHOUT imposing how you wanted me to grow. You showed us the importance of family! You showed me the diversity of the world. You always made yourself available. You usually gave me good advice! You get in all the clubs! You bought me a bed with mirrors.

MY LEGACY ACCORDING TO ROBIN

MY DAD HAS GREAT HAIR, AN OK SLAPSHOT, AND LOOKS GREAT IN A suit. He always made time for me, even when he should have been too busy. He doesn't cheat when we play golf—he's an honest scorekeeper. He always encouraged a balanced attack: education, sports, family, and fun. He has a great sense of humor and never takes himself too seriously. He loves with an open heart. He always believed in me and challenged me to learn more about my craft. He knows Hugh Hefner.

MY LEGACY ACCORDING TO CARTER (WHEN HE WAS FIVE):

I LOVE MY DAD BECAUSE HE BUYS ME TOYS. I LOVE HIM BECAUSE HE plays with me a lot. I love my dad because he lets me swing on the tree. I love him because he takes care of me. I love him because he loves me.

Raising a Rockstar

How to Guarantee Your Kid Will Be Rich and Famous

ONE MEASURE OF HOW SUCCESSFUL YOU'VE BEEN AS A PARENT IS whether or not you have to lie when people ask, "So, how are the kids?"

Sibling issues may need to be addressed if one child develops a more public, high-profile career. In this chapter, I'll write a little more about my middle son and that will suit my eldest just fine. In fact, he'd prefer it that way. Brennan chose not to be in the limelight after a brief but productive acting career. At age of twelve, he became the voice of Dennis the Menace in the remake of that cartoon series. Puberty killed that job when Brennan's voice suddenly dropped an octave and he started sounding like Darth Vader. Brennan cleverly segued into the music business when he became a DJ at age of fourteen, demonstrating to his little brother, Robin, how much fun music could be as a creative outlet, revenue stream, and chick magnet. Earlier, I mentioned his study at film school and I'm pleased to report that he and Robin now work together on movie scripts—Robin calls him "brilliant"—and, hopefully, you will see the fruits of their collaboration soon at a theatre near you.

Brennan has recently provided me with the ultimate Dad thrill: grandparenthood! My vanity refuses to give in easily to being called Grandpa—although I recognize the importance and privilege of that title.

I've enjoyed Robin calling me Pops. I love being called Dad by Brennan and Daddy by Carter. For the fabulous grandson, Tyler, I've considered Popster, Popperoni, Poppapalooza, PapaDooRunRun, PopTart, and Grampster. Maybe a combo old school/hip-hop name like Fuddy Diddy? Anyway, it's a work in progress, but we have some time before Tyler talks.

ON BECOMING BALDWIN

WE DON'T HAVE A ROYAL FAMILY IN THE AMERICAS. The Kennedys, Clintons, and Bushes come close to dynastic status but have made their coronation difficult with some questionable behavior on and off the job. The Baldwins are on the short list, but Daniel and Steven have diluted Alec's momentum by doing silly things. The Sheens are supremely talented but occasionally dysfunctional. At least Martin gets arrested for good intentions such as protesting oil spills...and Charlie's hit TV show is almost as entertaining as his real life.

Absent a Royal Family on which to focus our admiration as well as our gossip, jealousy, scorn, derision, and condescension, we have determined that in this country, celebrity of any origin—for any reason—is indeed the coin of the realm. Talent is not necessarily a prerequisite to celebrity: one extravagant performance in a badly lit but energetic sex tape can make you famous, guarantee a reality series, and lock up a perfume deal. It is this preoccupying fascination with fame that may inspire your children to choose the dreaded show business as a career.

If you're lucky, they might aim to become anchors at CNN or someplace where an education is required and not just a great butt, a fabulous rack, or model-like six-packs and chiseled "Good God!"-type looks.

The upside is that showbiz and broadcasting careers are not the Impossible (Pipe) Dreams they were once considered to be. The proliferation of cable and the Internet has created infinitely more opportunities for aspirants in communications and entertainment. There exists an entire industry devoted to keeping us posted on Britney's underwear and Lindsay's rehab...or who deserves to be president—and the Blitzers and Courics can't report forever. The Megan Foxes and Robert Pattinsons won't monopolize the "hot young thing" roles indefinitely. Schools can now more adequately prepare your children for these careers, and let's face it, job openings in land-based phone installation and analog television sales are going the way of the Maytag Man.

Still, there's no guarantee like the one nursing or plumbing careers provide.

"YES WE CAN"

NO ASPECT OF PUBLIC LIFE IS SEXIER THAN POPULAR MUSIC. OK, maybe the NBA, but I have no kids that tall.

Finding the delicate balance between supporting their dreams and cautioning against reality is key. Managers were all over Robin when he was sixteen and I was the wet-blanket realist who warned, to his occasional annoyance, that there was still a long road ahead. Even with his gift, there was a gestation period of several years with hype and promises from music producers, record labels, managers, and hordes of miscellaneous barnacles recognizing a gravy train when they see one. For those not familiar with my boy, shame on you. Please Google him. Now. I'll wait.

Thank you. Here's my update.

Robin Thicke had a big hit with a beautiful song called "Lost Without U." (He didn't learn spelling from me.) And his follow-up album was a smash! He was number one on the R&B charts for fourteen weeks. That's right: R&B as in "rhythm and blues." He is, admittedly, half Canadian and the list of Canadians who've punctured the Glass Funk Ceiling is short. (Other Canadians have succeeded at rhythm and blues...just not both...not at once...it's "either/or, take your pick, multiple choice, now let's dance!") What did I teach him? Nothing. His kind of talent skipped a generation.

COLLATERAL BENEFITS OF HEAT

I HAD TO FIGURATIVELY SPANK KIRK CAMERON FOR SEVEN years to meet women. Robin sings a ballad, touches his pants, and all hell breaks loose. He now has four bodyguards to fight off the same girls I used to pay guys to find.

"Advice" can be a two-way street for father and son. His advice to make me cooler has been to learn to say "get busy," not "make out," and the record will "drop," not be "released." I've been told that, "To roll with my crew, be down with my boo," which, roughly translated means, "You can't come to Vegas with us 'cause my wife is still mad about you puking on the carpet." I'm currently so "jonesing" to be "down" that now, when I want to "roll," I seek to do so with Robin's "crew, homey!" Of all the crewing and rolling I've ever done, this is the "baddest" and the "phattest." I am also reminded to keep my hands low when I dance because arms flailing in the air like a beekeeper on a bad day is apparently not sexy. His crew calls girls "shorty." I'll never be that hip.

My son's proudest "Dad moment" came when Snoop Dogg was asked on TV, "who was the weirdest celebrity you ever smoked reefer with?" When he answered, "Alan Thicke," Robin's phone started ringing off the hook. "Was that your dad or did Snoop mean you?" My explanation was simple: same party, second-hand smoke. Couldn't be me inhaling. I've tested positive for vanilla. Nevertheless, Robin was impressed. Kids today!

(Another note: Pot is now legal in California for "medical purposes." In L.A., medical purposes include getting through the day.)

WHERE WERE THE PARENTS?

WE'VE ALL HEARD THAT QUESTION WHEN IT'S REPORTED THAT Miley Cyrus took scandalous photos…or when Angelina famously tongued her brother…or when Drew Barrymore drank at ten and Danny Bonaduce did crack at fourteen. Our hearts go out to any actor named Corey and who among us is not afraid that Amy Winehouse may not survive? It's only a matter of time before one of the Jonas Brothers knocks up one of the Olsen sisters. Jamie-Lynn Spears became a baby mama at sixteen while older sister Britney crashed her car and had sex with a paparazzo—all on a custody day! Where was Mom? Oh yeah, Britney had a restraining order on hers.

Parenting by example is tricky if the examples are bad.

Hulk Hogan had a bad year. (His wife ran off with a nineteen-year-old, son went to jail for almost killing his friend in a car crash.) Hulk dealt with his grief by having an affair with his daughter's best friend.

David Archuleta's father had to be barred from the *American Idol* set.

Papa Lohan went to jail and Mama Dina should have for that reality show.

The parents of Aaron Carter and Macaulay Culkin should be Googled. Some say drawn and quartered.

Ashley and Mary-Kate wouldn't eat. Was Mom a lousy cook?

Gary Coleman's parents stole his frikkin' money!

KIDS GONE WILD

YOU NEVER KNOW WHEN YOUR KID COULD FREAK OUT AND BECOME a story on *Dateline*. "He was such a good boy, everybody liked him. We had no indication he might eat the neighbors." Because of that lifelong uncertainty, I WOULD NEVER DISPARAGE THE PARENTS OF TEENS WHO'VE RUN AMUCK because the kid's problems can never be entirely the parents' fault. Children themselves are culpable and "it takes a village" to screw up a prodigy.

We are the obvious, easy targets of blame, but believe me, you lose your leverage on behavior and control when your child is publicly beloved and independently wealthy. My guess is that Britney's dad had trouble getting her to tidy up her room at fourteen with her manager on the other line congratulating her for selling out Wembley Stadium. It's possible that Lionel Richie got tuned out when he scolded Nicole about her home-school geometry just as she was plotting to drop out and hook up with Heiress Paris for that unimaginably popular Bumpkin show.

How does a parent discipline or even "advise" a child who has money and sycophants before he can even spell "sychophants"? In the face of that kind of success and adulation, any youngster would feel "bulletproof." Your best hope is that they genuinely respect and value your opinion enough to seek your guidance because you have lost your power to threaten and deprive.

MONEY-BACK TIME

I WOULD LIKE TO NOW OFFER MY GUARANTEED GUIDELINES FOR making certain—inescapably, conclusively, and inevitably—that your son or daughter will succeed if their target is the music industry. I would like to, but I cannot.

Unfortunately I know of no such irrefutable formula, so this chapter can end right here. Unless, of course, you would care to hear some vague, broader observations on the subject of cultivating a "can't-miss" rocker. The fact is there are no sure-fire roadmaps, but here are the Top 10 Tips to improve your odds.

1) MUSIC LESSONS

Don't force kids to take them. That can be a turn-off and poison your child for life against the whole idea. They'll come to you if they're interested enough to hone technique.

2) EXPOSURE

Make sure they hear all sorts of music. Change happens quickly and the "next big thing" soon becomes the "ex-big thing." Drawing on a variety of influences and genres will formulate a less derivative musical personality. After all, "fusion" is how we got rock 'n' roll in the first place, how rap became hip-hop, and how mainstream pop has expanded through the influence of Latin beats…and jazz, by definition, is always part of musical evolution.

Instead of brow-beating them into lessons, take your children to concerts and musicals; display your own joy in the performance and the effect will be contagious…unless they can't stand you and would rather do anything than be like you and share your dorky pursuits.

My "gift" to Robin was that, as a music lover and fan myself, I took him to concerts ranging from Run DMC to Gordon Lightfoot…Prince to Anne Murray to Bob Seger to the Beastie Boys, the Eagles, the Bee Gees, and so on.

3) ARTISTRY, NOT CELEBRITY

That tabloid/paparazzi/TMZ/YouTube ride lasts about as long as a pimple. True Art, on the other hand, will rekindle and flourish for a lifetime regardless of fads and trends. Genuine skill—whether in visual, literary, musical, or performance art—will serve you longer than your "sexy factor." Those who pay the price of excellence, who invest the time and have the passion to learn their craft will be around long after the trunk droops, the rack wrinkles, and the spotlight shifts.

4) TRUNK AND RACK MAINTENANCE

Nevertheless, physical conditioning is essential to a long-term career on stage. Robin has the body of a pro athlete. By the time your rockstar is touring and dancing in videos, he or she will need all the flexibility and stamina they can muster. Taking great physical care of oneself—notwithstanding some notably bad examples—helps the high achievers avoid throat problems, groin pulls, fatigue, mood swings, and the resultant cancelled concerts, flaky reputations, and early burnouts that plague many unsuspecting, unprepared pretenders.

5) TIGHT GENES

Don't rely on—or worry about—the trickle-down effect of genetics. Ignore the Heredity vs. Environment Intelligent Design Argument as relates to pop music.

The most remarkable thing about Robin's musical talent is that it is self-inflicted. There is probably some hereditary component to musicality the same way genetic musculature and skeletal structuring must contribute to one's athleticism. But he only inherited six chords from me, the other stuff he found on his own. Even more remarkable is that he's self-taught on the technical side. Although he was a reliable B student—one of those kids who did well with minimal effort—he showed no predilection for computer skills in high school. Definitely no genetic help there; I still marvel at automatic transmissions and color TV. It amazes me that he can command a recording studio's synthesized sounds and infinite mixing possibilities with such facility and confidence. Music is a good reason to encourage your child's computer skills.

My most important career advice for him was to "write," since that's where longevity and dollars live, and because "old songwriters never die, they just decompose."

6) THE ONLY BOX REFERENCE

Challenge what's known. Nothing new comes from thinking old. If you don't teach yourself something that no one else can, "You won't create, you'll just regurgitate." (Jesse Jackson may use that one!)

Nothing unique or revolutionary will come from a person who can't think "outside the box." I detest that expression but I can't think far enough outside the box to come up with a new cliché. Respect the past, learn from it, but don't be limited by it.

7) "NICE" CAN BE COOL

Apart from his obvious skill, I am especially proud of Robin's demeanor when I hear from people at shows he's appeared on such as *Oprah*, *Letterman*, *Leno*, *Jimmy Kimmel*, *Ellen*, *Regis & Kelly*—and not just the stars but the worker bees on set—that he's a gentleman who treats people properly. "Be nice to people on your way up 'cause you'll meet the same ones on the way down." Conversely, I'm always happy to hear that I've left a legacy of fondness in those circles—Robin usually hears that Dad did his job and didn't piss anybody off. Too much. Not very often. Maybe once in a while.

I am tickled at the "Robin Love" I feel in public places, walking through restaurants and hearing, "Hey, that's Robin Thicke's dad!" (It was, "Hey, Kirk Cameron's dad!" for years so I was ready for the real thing.) I've been pulled aside at parties by icons who took the time to tell me how much they love my boy's work. Stevie Wonder, Whitney Houston, Mary J., Kanye, Mother Teresa, Madame Curie, and Franklin Delano Roosevelt. (I sometimes exaggerate when I'm name-dropping, but if you're a proud parent you understand.) When I hear "Robin Love" from Mr. Springsteen, my life will be complete.

One of his biggest fans is little brother, Carter, who has shown a keen interest in guitar. Robin's intelligent advice to him has been that "talent" is "gift plus effort." Simple. True.

As gratifying as a productive career is to oneself, it is surely one of life's great rewards when your child does it. "You complete me," indeed!

8) NO CHILD LEFT BEHIND

Robin decided not to attend college on the grounds that the music industry is demographically driven and anyone starting out at the age of twenty-one is probably too old, too dated, and too destined to mediocrity. I reluctantly concurred and he was able to go from high school to ROCKSTAR immediately...if you consider fifteen years to be immediate. As his education, he paid his dues writing and producing for others: Christina Aguilera, Pink, Usher, Brian McKnight, Jennifer Hudson, Lil Wayne, 50 Cent, Pharrel, Francis Scott Key, Thomas Edison, and John Phillip Sousa, just to name a few. OK, I may have hyperbolized again but when I get in my "name-dropping" rhythm, I can't be stopped. At least, that's what Elvis told me.

A great way to learn your business is to be in the company of greatness—of successful people who've gone before.

9) ...

OK, that's only eight tips. Maybe some other parent can help you with two more. Harry Connick SENIOR?

THE GREAT WORK IN PROGRESS

AT THE BEGINNING, I OFFERED MY CREDENTIALS FOR RELEASING a book with this title, but I believe my best boast would be testimonials from my own children. I have, in fact, raised three kids who don't hate me. Not that they always agree with me, respect me, and obey me, but we "get" each other, and it's all good. My two grown guys have both achieved success in their chosen fields of rock 'n' roll and real estate. That's not what we used to refer to as the three R's, but it's worked for them. My daily prayer continues to be for their health and happiness—riches and fame are nice but optional—and of course, the old, reliable "Making a Difference," which should be on every parent's wish list for his children. And we should all be honest enough to recognize that we want the package to include the assurance that they do indeed love us. Their love is why we're here—it defines our very existence, and nothing will ever come before it.

I hope these pages have convinced you that we can leave our children a better world and given you confidence that the generation that follows can, indeed, improve on the one that went before it. "Don't do as I do, or even as I say, but do something better than I ever did." Encourage your children to raise the bar, and you'll be thrilled when they do just that.

Good friends are important. I always encouraged my kids to bring their friends over, and I knew their friends' names and welcomed them. They liked that. If I taught them anything, I hope they learned that in life, family comes first—always. My kids laugh a lot, joke a lot, hug a lot. They learned that from me. I like that.

HOW BRENNAN TURNED OUT

MY FIRSTBORN LIVES AROUND THE CORNER. WE TALK EVERY DAY, and I have never said a prayer in twenty-five years that does not begin with, "Please cure Brennan's diabetes," just so God always knows where I stand in case I only get one wish. Great kid.

Big winner. Thanks, God. (Now, about that diabetes…)

HOW ROBIN TURNED OUT

RATHER THAN SIMPLY CONTINUING TO PLAY THE BRAGGING FATHER, let me quote these record industry insiders:

- "The closest we're going to come to Stevie Wonder." (*Rolling Stone*)
- "Marvin Gaye backed by Radiohead." (*Interview* Magazine)
- "Bright, committed, sensitive, funny, caring, socially conscious guy." (Me)

Robin has been described as "Malibu meets Harlem." I'd say Eminem without the mother-slapping. (At seventeen, I learned to play the guitar so I could meet girls. I only knew four chords, because the girls you'd meet with five chords would be too smart and that would defeat the purpose. Besides, more than four chords was considered jazz on the '60s scene, and I was a nuts-and-bolts rocker at heart.)

My boys' real musical lineage goes back to Grandma Issie, who played piano for the silent movies in Kirkland Lake, circa 1925. That's where she met Will, an usher in the town theater, and that, after all, is how our family got here.

ON MARRYING UP

AS A FINAL UPDATE ON THE FAMILY FORTUNES, I'D RECOMMEND that your children marry "up," as my boys have done by snagging winners. Brennan's wife, Kathleen ("Dolly"), designs wedding dresses and Mrs. Robin Thicke, Paula Patton (fab actress) was the inspiration for "Lost Without U," which made its debut at my wedding to Tanya. Not a dry seat in the house after that.

As for Tanya…no one has married more "up" than me.

FROM THE AUTHOR

MAY YOU ALL BE AS BLESSED AS I HAVE BEEN TO KNOW THE LOVE and joy that only children can bring. And please take time to enjoy the ride!

Thanks for listening and sincere best wishes always,

– Alan

MORE FAMILY PHOTOS

Brennan and Kathleen's Wedding

Dad Gets Married!

Wedding Celebration

Made for Each Other

Front Porch with Tanya and Carter

Home Sweet Home

I guess Robin took this picture...

Brennan and Dolly gave me Grandson Tyler!

Tanya and Alan

About the Author

WITH FIVE EMMY NOMINATIONS FOR COMEDY WRITING, a syndicated humor column in Canada, an amusing book about fathering (*How Men Have Babies: The Pregnant Father's Survival Guide*), and a reputation as one of TV's favorite dads in the acclaimed sitcom *Growing Pains*, Alan Thicke has created an enduring comedic legacy in the world of entertainment.

"Alan is funny in life. I've been there through weddings, divorces, births, passages, successes, and setbacks. He has a way of seeing reality for what it is, dealing with it, and finding the humor in it. He really loves his family, and he'll make you laugh with yours."

– Steven Shore, agent, manager, confidant, and longtime friend